An Illustrated Historical Survey

of the

RAILWAYS IN AND AROUND

BURY

by
Jeffrey Wells

Dedicated to Gillian and Stephen

Acknowledgements

Throughout the preparation of this book, I have been fortunate to be able to enlist the help and guidance of many knowledgeable people. Without their interest and co-operation, the task of compiling the finished article would have been impossible. I visited several libraries and organisations is search of material and at each one found the staff and volunteers more than willing to spend time pointing me in the right direction, finding a spot for me to work in, and occasionally finding an unusual item of interest which had lain undisturbed for perhaps many years.

Many thanks are due to Bacup Library, Bacup Natural History Society, Bolton Central Library, Bury Central Library, Greater Manchester Record Office, Middleton Library the National Railway Museum, Radcliffe Library, Ramsbottom Heritage Centre, Ramsbottom Library, and the Salford Mining Museum.

Many individual people have contributed to the success of the project. I am very grateful to Brenda Decent, Michael Blakemore and Peter Morgan who allowed me to borrow valuable photographs. Thanks are also due to Alex Appleton, Fred Collinge, Gordon Coltas, Ray Farrell, David Mills, Don Steggles, Frank Sunderland and Tom Wray, all of whom furnished either photographs or information, or both, in my quest for details and illustrative material. Also those photographers who are credited alongside the captioned illustrations - thanks. I am equally grateful to Robert Proctor for his help in highlighting DMU details, and to David Smith who unstintingly spent his time giving me a 'guided tour' of the Rawtenstall to Bacup route during the Spring of 1993. Richard Greenwood read the proofs with an eagle-eye and added much besides taking me to task on a number of points for which I am indebted.

I would like to record here my gratitude to the Bury Times Newspaper Group which printed my request for local information from readers. To those who took the trouble to reply, I owe much, especially to Don Battersby, Margaret and Eric Nadin, and Fred Williams.

Last but not least, a mention must be made of Jim Murphy who, not for the first time, has provided his photographic skills, and Tim Baker-Jones at W.H Smith Archives.

CHALLENGER PUBLICATIONS

Introduction

It was at the invitation of the publisher that I began to delve into the railways of Bury and its environs. I set myself the task of covering a wide area of ground, from Bury to Bacup, Broadfield to Bradley Fold, and the neighbouring town of Radcliffe, where so much existed and occurred yet with little written in recognition of the fact. The LYR Manchester to Bury electrification scheme and its progenitor, the Holcombe Brook branch, also form part of the story. In the former, I have concentrated on the pioneering aspects; in the latter, a full description of the route with the elements of its history have been covered.

Amongst the many sources of printed information, reference has been made to O.S. 1:2500 plans of 1937 vintage, these furnishing details of central Bury and the disposition of the routes covered, coinciding with a period of maturity under LMS management and before the first hints of decline post 1945.

Wherever possible, an attempt has been made to reconstruct events as seen through the eyes of newspaper reports, official reports and contemporary observers, and with the aid of verbal details provided by those fortunate enough to have the advantage of direct knowledge.

The research and writing of this book has been both educational and rewarding and the hope is that my enthusiasm (which grew apace the more I discovered) shines through the text, and that the illustrations give nostalgic pleasure of what used to be. *JW 1994*

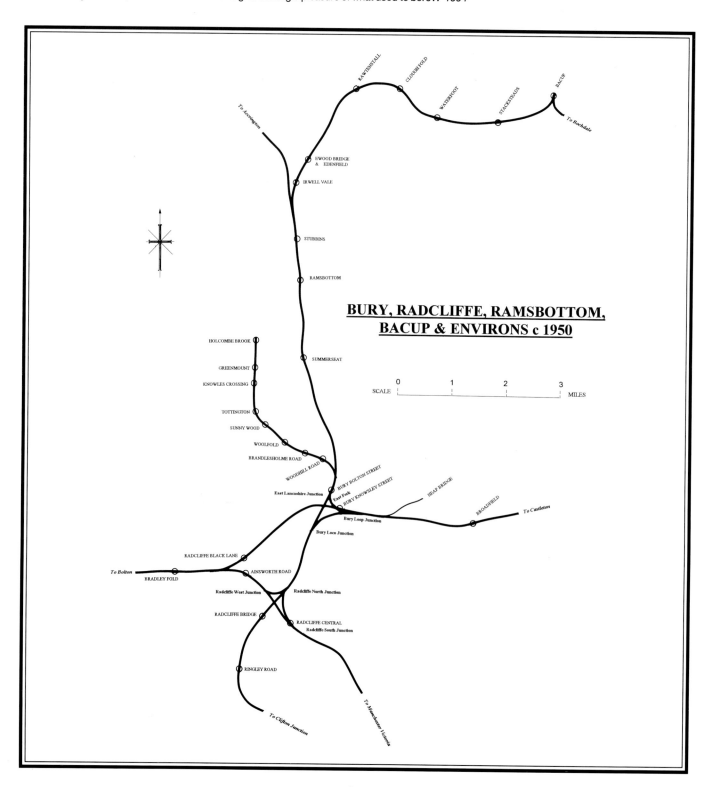

BURY, RADCLIFFE, RAMSBOTTOM, BACUP & ENVIRONS c 1950

Chapter 1. THE EARLY RAILWAYS THROUGH BURY

"The district has much traffic with Manchester, Liverpool and the rest of the kingdom for which at present there is no means of transit save by hilly and inconvenient roads and by very circuitous canal navigation. Each year increases the extent of this traffic...."
Contemporay 19th century newspaper quotation.

The South - North Route - The first railway to approach the vicinity of Bury was the Manchester Bolton & Bury Navigation & Railway Company, a long-winded title for a railway which had been forged out of an effort to stave off railway competition with the existing Manchester, Bolton & Bury Canal (a threat to the latter came from the Bolton & Leigh Railway and the Liverpool & Manchester Railway). The directors of the canal, led by their chairman Sir John Tobin, had made a decision to convert their canal into a railway and to this end, obtained an Act of Parliament on 23rd August 1831. Several proposals were made, and after several changes of mind, the decision to build a railway, not alongside or on the in-filled canal, but between Salford and Bolton by way of Pendleton, Dixon Fold, Kearsley and Farnworth. The original intention had been to extend a branch to Bury but this never materialised, having suffered opposition from the start by the company's engineer Jesse Hartley. According to John Marshall, the Bury branch would have called for a 1,100 yard tunnel on a gradient of 1 in 100, at the time an expensive and daunting engineering task. However, Hartley's idea of three tracks, one for goods and two for passenger traffic, also never materialised, only two tracks being laid. Thus, the nearest point that the railway made with Bury was at Stoneclough, some 4½ miles to the south west.

The Manchester to Bolton line opened for public use on 29th May 1838, leaving Bury isolated from a railway connection with the outside world. By the early 1840's, the need for a railway connection with its larger neighbour to the south, "Cottonopolis" (Manchester), was again held imperative. The well-known story has often been recounted where "influential people" met in the Red Lion hostelry in Bury to decide upon the best way of securing Bury's railway route. This meeting was convened on the 14th September 1843 and included such influential persons as John Grundy, Thomas Wrigley, John Kay and others. The object of the meeting was fulfilled: a new company taking the title of The Manchester, Bury & Rossendale Railway was formed. Its purpose was to construct a double track railway from Clifton, so forming a junction with the Manchester and Bolton line. The plan, however, was far more ambitious than a line running from Clifton to Bury. The company promoted the idea of the line continuing northwards from Bury along the Irwell Valley to reach Rawtenstall via Ramsbottom.

With this intention fully underway, another company, The Blackburn, Burnley, Accrington & Colne Extension Railway proposed to continue the line from Stubbins Junction (between Ramsbottom and Rawtenstall) northwards to meet the west-to-east Preston to Burnley route at Accrington. So well did the two railways knit together that the two companies amalgamated to form the East Lancashire Railway by Act of Parliament on 24th July 1845. This co-joining of the two companies was an example of what Grote Lewin termed an "end-on" amalgamation - both original companies subscribing to the East Lancashire Railway and representing a consolidation of interests which had always been intended.

In her MA Thesis (1974) *An Historical Geography of South Rossendale*, Stephanie Harrison considered the purchase of land by the MB&RR between Bury and Rawtenstall, and found that there had been no great problem in purchasing land. Tithe Surveys had shown that the land along the projected route was made up of "waste, woodland, pasture or reservoirs, except at Brooksbottoms where arable land was avoided by the tunnel". Built-up land was rare in this predominantly rural area, and where it did occur, it was "classified more strictly". The route of the railway carefully "avoided Square Mill and Ramsbottom Mill", the company not wishing to inflame the good will of the mill owners or to incur heavy legal and compensation expenses. "But prices differed between parties. Lord Derby, in contrast with other sellers, received £400 per statute acre for agricultural land" whereas a Mr Cooper claimed £200 per statute acre and 5 shillings per yard for building land at Stubbins. In contrast with the Extension line to Accrington, there were few instances where the Company had to resort to legal arbitration and compulsory purchase. Most of the occupations of the shareholders (77%) had been shown to be involved in local trade and industry. "Among the landowners were Richard Hamer (although not a shareholder), John Robinson Kay, William Grant & Brothers and Messrs Ashton, all classified in local Directories as manufacturers or merchants". The landed interest alone was "relatively unimportant", with the exception of Lord Derby who was certainly not a manufacturer or merchant!

The route along the Irwell valley was surveyed by General Pasley on 23rd September 1846. The divergence of the line to Rawstenstall and the extension to Accrington occurred at the village of Stubbins, forever afterwards to be known as Stubbins Junction, and in effect reduced the former line to a branch line status.

An early view of Knowsley Street station depicting the scene shortly after its opening. Dominating the scene is Knowsley Street bridge whilst beyond is Manchester Road bridge, complete with stagecoach, and a train approaching off Bury East Fork. The distant third bridge, complete with train, takes the Bolton Street - Manchester line across the Bolton line. *Bury Central Library.*

The Clifton to Rawtenstall contract had been awarded to Pauling & Henfrey, a Manchester firm of contractors, in May 1844. These contractors had been building new barracks on Bolton Road in Bury and with John Hawkshaw's recommendation, their tender of £167,529 was readily accepted as two separate contracts: Clifton to Bury and Bury to Rawtenstall/Accrington. In July 1844, the *Manchester Guardian* was moved to report that :

> "The works on this important line have been commenced with great spirit in Outwood Clough, the remainder of the line is being railed off and the bustle of preparation is observable on every hand".

Such large scale contracts were normally sub-let to smaller contractors who were involved in smaller sections of the work. For example John Kellett had men working at Radcliffe; John Caldwell at Touchy Hill; John Heywood at Nuttall Tunnel.

William Harrison, looking back in 1882, wrote of the commendable speed at which the work was carried out: "The railway was speedily completed and was opened for traffic on 28th September 1846". Not before, of course, the mandatory Board of Trade inspection in that year by General Pasley who cast his critical eye over the line between Clifton and Rawtenstall (14 miles) and found much to his satisfaction. "He expressed himself very highly pleased with the good substantial character of the works". *Manchester Guardian 26th Sept.1846.*

General Pasley may have been 'highly pleased' but the finished product he had inspected had also had its share of difficulties. The summer of 1845 had brought a paucity of workers, such was the spread of engineering work in progress. Not to be dismayed, men were asked to work on Sunday. The *Manchester Guardian* reported on 30th July 1845 that seven men had been charged with breaking the Sabbath. The winter of 1845/6 brought continuous wet weather which hindered progress: there were landslips and embankments would not hold up due to the mixture of clay and sand, the latter easily washed away as quickly as it was tipped. If this was not enough, the recommended contractors Pauling & Henfrey were charged with misleading the Company on the amount of time needed to construct the line. Their apparent lack of progress led to their dismissal, the contract given to John Waring, the equipment of the former being seized by way of compensation.

The usual procedure before the public opening of a railway was to run a train on a special service, conveying company and town officials, along with invited guests and other interested parties. This was done on Friday, 25th September 1846 with great jubilation and a holiday atmosphere prevailing along the railway. Thousands lined the route, and by the time the special had reached its destination, Rawtenstall, over 600 passengers detrained to enjoy "an elegant collation" inside the newly erected weaving shed of John Robinson Kay.

The Proposed Atmospheric Railway - The construction of the East Lancashire Railway between Clifton Junction and Rawtenstall occurred at the height of the so-called Railway Mania. Townspeople in Bury also sought the opportunity to link their town directly with Manchester, and much to the irritation of the ELR, a proposed Manchester and Bury Atmospheric Railway was announced in September 1845. This Company's Prospectus was published in the Manchester Guardian on 8th October 1845 and revealed to all the raison d'etre for the scheme:

> "Considering the amount of traffic carried between the two towns (Manchester and Bury) and intermediate places, no locality could be pointed out where a direct railway is more urgently needed. This has evidently been proved by the warm reception the scheme has met with at both termini and from inhabitants locally interested"

The railway was to commence at Hunt's Bank, Manchester and then pass through Broughton, Cheetham Hill and Prestwich before termination at the Market Place in Bury. A petition in support of the Atmospheric Railway was presented to Parliament on the 8th February 1846 but withdrawn shortly afterwards. "...because of the joint opposition of the ELR and the MLR, and also the opposition of the Earl of Derby" *Manchester Guardian 25th July 1846.*

The Atmospheric Railway Company wound up that month, and with hindsight, this was as well, considering the final failure of Brunel's experiment with the atmospheric system in South Devon.

The East-West Route. - From the public opening of the Liverpool & Manchester Railway on the 15th September 1830, rail communication between the Irish Seaport and East Lancashire lay in the hands of this famous company - a disliked monopolistic situation in some quarters. Passengers between Liverpool and Manchester did, however, have the benefit of a direct route, but intermediate journeys were awkward. Marshall cites the example of journeys between Bolton and Wigan, a

The driver's eye view of the east face of Manchester Road bridge on 25th May 1970. The view has been taken from beneath Knowsley Street bridge and clearly shows the commencement of 'Bury Hollow' where the Bolton lines dipped under the Clifton Junction to Bolton Street line (the overbridge can be seen in the distance). Curving off to the right is the East Fork, the sharply curved and inclined link to Bolton Street station. Compare this latter day view with that on the previous page.*Tom Wray.*

4

relatively short distance of 9 miles, where passengers had to travel by way of Kenyon Junction via the Grand Junction Railway, along the L & M to Parkside Junction and then via the North Union Railway's line to Wigan, a distance of 19 miles!

By 1840, it was felt that a change was necessary and the L & M monopoly had to be broken. As early as 1834, it had been suggested by interested parties, that a branch off the then proposed Manchester, Bolton & Bury Railway to Liverpool would be suitable, and a route was actually surveyed by a Mr. Comrie. However, as with many other schemes throughout the land, the idea never materialised.

As in the case of the Manchester, Bolton & Bury Railway, the impetus behind the formation to break the existing 'situation' sprang from a group of businessmen in Liverpool, Wigan and Bolton. This included some influential people: the Earl of Balcarras, Sir Thomas Brancker, and a host of others with interests in Wigan, Bolton, Liverpool and Manchester. The whole scheme started with a capital of £800 000 in 16,000 shares of £50 each.

The first germ of an idea to link Liverpool with Wigan and Bolton appeared in the *Bolton Free Press* on 12th October 1844, and read;

> "The public are respectfully informed that it is intended to apply in the next session of Parliament powers to form a direct Railway Communication between the towns of Bolton, Wigan and Liverpool, passing through the important Coal district of Upholland, and terminating near the North Docks in Liverpool. Provisional Committee - Henry Gaskell & S.D.Derbyshire"

A further Prospectus appeared in the same newspaper on the 19th October 1844 which outlined a proposal to extend the line beyond Bolton to Bury and Rochdale:

> "The Provisional Committee have it in contemplation to Extend this Undertaking to Bury and Heywood, with a view to give direct railway communication between the important towns of Rochdale, Heywood, Bury, Bolton and Wigan and more fully to extend to these places the advantage of the original scheme. They have reason to believe that a moderate increase of the capital will enable them to accomplish this important objective. Henry Gaskell, Wigan; S.D.Derbyshire, Manchester".

The title of this nascent railway company changed to the Liverpool & Bury Railway, a name which was to hold from its inception by Act of Parliament on the 31st August 1845 until its amalgamation with the Manchester and Leeds Railway by an Act of 27th July 1846.

The outcome of the Liverpool to Bury line was the extension beyond Bury to Heywood where it would join the Manchester & Leeds branch from Castleton. However, this continuation eastwards was refused and had to wait until the Manchester & Leeds absorbed the Liverpool & Bury. As with the fortunes of the Manchester, Bury & Rossendale Railway, events changed quickly and at times overtook current work in progress. By an Act of 9th July 1847, the Manchester & Leeds, one of the foremost early railway companies, metamorphosed into the Lancashire & Yorkshire Railway. The same Act also authorised the Liverpool to Bury route to continue to Heywood so that there would now be a continuous route from Liverpool to Yorkshire. On a local level, the same Act authorised an east to north curve so joining the west to east route with the south to north. This curve was located between Bury's two stations, the ELR's Bolton Street and the Lancashire & Yorkshire's Knowsley Street (or Bury Station as it was then known), opened to the public on 20th November 1848.

The *Manchester Guardian* of 3rd May 1848 paid tribute to the line's opening in the following way, referring particularly to the "Heywood Railway" between Blue Pits and Bury:-

> "On Monday last the branch of the Lancashire & Yorkshire Railway completing the communication (by that company's lines) between Manchester and Bury, was opened. The trains commenced running at eight o'clock in the morning, and con-

tinued to do so during the day. At half-past two o'clock Mr.Barnes (one of the directors), the secretary, engineer, treasurer, and other officers of the company proceeded in one of the trains to Bury, where they were met by several gentlemen of that town, and partook of a cold collation at the invitation of the latter. The distance between Manchester and Bury by this line will be thirteen miles; the portion newly opened, consisting of four miles, from Heywood to Bury, together with a short branch of about a mile in length from the main line of the Lancashire & Yorkshire Railway at Blue Pits to the Heywood Branch in order to enable trains from Manchester to get up the line without backing. It is intended to run from Manchester to Bury in half-an-hour, which is the time occupied in going between the two places by the East Lancashire line.... The only station between Heywood and Bury will be Heap Bridge. The works of the newly-completed branch are rather heavy, as the country through which it runs is of a boldly undulating character. There are several embankments, cuttings, and bridges, all of which have been constructed entirely to the satisfaction of the Government Inspector. There are no tunnels..... The new line forms the link of communication between Manchester and the Liverpool and the Bury line.....".

The two routes, west to east and north to south were not allowed to intersect on the level, (Section 16 of the 31st July 1845 Act had prevented this), so that the Liverpool to Bury line had to dip beneath the ELR line a short distance west of Knowsley Street Station locally known as 'The Hump' (in L&Y official records it was also called "the Hollow"). Authorisation to do so had been granted as part of the Act of 19th July 1847. The east to west route was 40 miles long between Castleton and Liverpool, laid as double track throughout, and opened fully to passenger and goods traffic in December 1848, following the customary B.O.T. inspection carried out by Captain Wynne during the previous month.

Engineering work in the Bury area included several bridges and viaducts which were required to cross the rivers Roch and Irwell. To the east of Bury, at Pimhole, a timber viaduct over the Roch had been erected around 1847/1848 in order to carry the Manchester and Leeds extension from Heywood to Bury. The latter was only 3 miles and 6 furlongs throughout and yet took two years to complete. The *Manchester Guardian* of 12th June 1847, after extolling the work of the contractor, George Thomson, described the work at Pimhole in which,

> "..... an enormous embankment was required to carry the line towards the viaduct over the River Roch - the quality of the earth, being sand and loam, taken from a deep cutting at Spout Bank, was unfavourable to embankment making".

The timber viaduct was replaced in brick by the LYR for £3,491. During its construction, single line working was in operation which, on one occasion, the 8th November 1862, involved a minor accident in fog. The *Manchester Guardian* reported the incident under the following sub-headline,

> "Fog in East Lancashire - Increased vigilance at Roche (sic) Viaduct at Pimhole, still under construction, to prevent accident. The 11.29 special service from Bury to Manchester detained at the viaduct until the train from Normanton to Liverpool had passed. Whilst the train was waiting, the train from Normanton to Liverpool came up and ran into the Bury train at a reduced speed. Many of the passengers were much shaken".

The viaduct was completed on 11th November 1862 without further incident.

To the west of Bury, the railway had to cross both the River Irwell as it flowed south towards Radcliffe and the Manchester, Bolton & Bury Canal, the course of which ran alongside the river. This was accomplished by erecting a stone viaduct of five arches, each of 73ft span, over the two water courses.

Chapter 2. CENTRAL BURY

"To estimate the effect of the railway upon the social and economic life of a town such as Bury, so closely interwoven as it was with its neighbours and dominated by the nearby giant of Manchester, would be extremely difficult.... for unlike Brighton or Blackpool, Bury was not an isolated village prior to the railways"
The Railway Comes to Bury . Harry Hanson 1969.

The date was the 25th September 1846. The inauguration of the East Lancashire Railway was marked by a special train which conveyed railway and town dignatories from the Victoria Station, Manchester to the bucolic station at Rawtenstall. To enhance the journey, the 5th Regiment of Foot military band played popular airs as the large and distinguished ensemble, drawn by a 2-2-2 locomotive, made its way into Bury, arriving at 1.15 p.m., the first-ever train to enter the town and halt there.

The travellers found themselves amidst a large building site, the incomplete ELR station lying just off Bolton Street, hemmed in a slot in the ground by high stone revetments. The future Company headquarters, in the first stages of construction, (it was to be a three-storey brick and stone building) was beginning to rise from its foundations amongst a pile of bricks, stone and mortar, trestles and ladders, and all the accoutrement of the building trade.

These early travellers by train, caught up in the exhilaration of something new, something different and long-awaited, how could they have imagined how the town's railway future was to evolve? A short distance from Bolton Street station, the Liverpool & Bury Railway had been striking through Bury from west to east and its new station site, adjacent to John Street (later Knowsley Street) was already established, though the station was not to open for a further 26 months. Both railways had made a physical impact on parts of the Town during construction, tunnelling, excavating, disturbing existing properties, stopping off streets and closing premises by compulsory purchase. In full maturity, the railway presence in Bury embraced two stations, an engine shed, a carriage works, a wagon works, several goods yards, private sidings and a network of routes which gave the town a long cherished connection with the outside world.

Bolton Street station frontage circa 1900. An interesting scene revealing several details of the station as it appeared from the street, and its position there. First, the frontage imposed itself on the street with its eye-catching turret clock and distinctive valence. Note the heavy iron gates which were hung on massive stone columns at the entrance to the inclined roadway into the station yard. Secondly, beyond the station, is the gable end of a shop - Mr Ambler's hatters and outfitter, at No's. 26 and 27 Bolton Street. This is the shop often referred to in the construction of the very first and temporary Bolton Street station. Two horse-drawn cabs await custom outside the station, and amongst the other horse-drawn traffic, a lone motor car heads towards the town centre. *LYR Society Collection.*

The aim of this chapter is to look at the development of Bury's railway infrastructure and to describe the fabric as it was when it full-flourished and before there was hint of demise and loss. Let us begin with the stations, for they were the focal points in which the vast majority of people came face-to-face with Bury's railways.......

Bolton Street Station (also known as "Bury EL" and `Bury High Level') - It appears that soon after the inaugural train, a public service began, a temporary station, situated behind the Lord Nelson Inn and a Mr Ambler's shop, being reached by a steeply sloping path from street level. The *Manchester Guardian* of 26th September 1846, dutifully reported that the railway

> ".... will be opened to the public on Monday next, September 28th ..... The station is in the course of erection, and will be fitted up with refreshment rooms and private apartments..... the line is double as far as Bury, and single up to Stubbins Bridge; but between these points there is a double line of rails, one of which is used by the contractor for carrying their works....."

It was sometime later, possibly 23rd August 1847, that the permanent Bolton Street station was completed, and again, the *Manchester Guardian* of 28th July 1849 informed its readers that,

> "The company offices and station house is a handsome brick edifice with stone dressings, on the right of the line, three storeys in height, with a frontage of 180 feet; and consisting of a centre portion, 24 feet deep, and two connecting wings, each 32 feet square. The station ground is not yet completed. It is roofed over for a length of 274 feet; the roof is light, being of iron lined with inch board, the central ridge on both sides being of horticultural glass. The roof springs from the office buildings, on the east side of the line; on the west side, it is supported by fifteen cast iron columns. The station is well lighted at night, by sixteen octagonal gas lanterns. There are three passenger platforms; the principal one adjoining the offices, for the trains north (sic) is of stone, 280 feet long, and 16 feet wide; the centre one (between the two lines of rail) is a wooden step platform, about 200 feet in length, for the Accrington trains; there is a third platform of wood, on the west side of the line, about the same length, for the trains south..... Beyond the station shed on the west side, are the lines or sidings for the Up and Down goods trains which are thus kept wholly apart from the passenger trains... At each end of the offices is a roofed carriage shed; the north one is 185 feet long, the south one about 10 feet shorter... The carriage building shops are opposite the station and general offices on the west side of the line..... north of the tunnel (under Bolton Street) is a coal stage east of the line, and an extensive goods warehouse west of it...."

As already mentioned, the station and yard were confined within stone retaining walls of some 20-25 ft height, the wall on the eastern side stopped in two places, and breached by a set of stone steps leading up to Bank Street. The latter represented a street truncated by the railway; it originally connected with Irwell Street on the western side of the station. During excavation of the yard, Bank Street Unitarian Chapel

A close-up of Bolton Street station frontage in the 1920's. The turret clock is still in place as is the ornate valence, and now there is an additional sign announcing "Bolton Street Station". Close examination reveals the initials "LMS" on bill boards which would suggest the pivotal year 1923 when the vestiges of the LYR continued for a time with the new order of things. Wall signs extreme left inform of the availability of seasonal tickets for use on the electric train service. Fares given for Crumpsall: 9d 1st class, 6½d 3rd class; Woodlands Road: 10d 1st class, 8½d 3rd class; Manchester Victoria: 1/4d 1st class?, 8d 3rd class?. *LYR Society Collection.*

was undermined, a situation which inflamed the church authorities and which led to legal action the outcome of which forced the ELR to provide a new Unitarian church, at No.6 Bank Street. This was just one of the many irritating problems encountered by the ELR in driving a railway through an urban area; and is akin to the construction of motorways in an urban area today.

The station continued in its original form with minor modifications until a decision to rebuild was taken by the LYR in the 1880s. The refurbished station was completed in 1883 as the following account reveals, appearing in the *Manchester Guardian* 12th May 1883: "The Lancashire and Yorkshire Railway Company have almost completed a

new station at Bury at a cost of from £10,000 to £12,000. The platforms have been raised and lengthened and now extend 250 yards. On the down island platform are new waiting rooms. The new station is carried over the line and faces Bolton Street, being set back to all carriages to put down passengers at the door of the Booking Office. The passengers descend by a covered approach to an overbridge, which leads to either platform without the necessity of crossing the lines as before. The approach and overbridge are roofed in and glazed and the station and approaches are lighted with Bray's lamps. The works have been carried out by Mr.Charles Brierley, builder, Bury."

The LYR removed the original train shed roof and in its place provided protection by erecting a canopy over both platforms, the one over the Down platform being the longer and supported by two rows of cast iron columns. The shorter Up platform canopy was attached for most of its length to the ELR 'office block' and also supported by columns. In LYR and LMS days, the track layout was as follows: two through lines, Up and Down, serving platforms 2 and 3 respectively, a loop line on the west side serving platform 4, (a kick-back siding ran off this back to Tenterden Street bridge), and a bay siding on the Up side, serving platform 1 with a loading dock alongside it.

Access to the station could be made via the main booking office on Bolton Street (the booking office stood on the left of the booking hall, with a W.H.Smith bookstall on the right on entering). Another entrance could be made by way of a sloping setted driveway down to a set of iron gates, beyond which was a ticket collector's cabin guarding a small side entrance to the Up platform.

Amenities on the ground floor of the old ELR building were well-provided for both railway staff and passengers: these included waiting

(below) **Platforms 3 and 2, Bolton Street, 24th April 1951. An ex-LYR three-car e.m.u. stands at platform 2 with unit M28514 at the Manchester end. This was originally numbered 3516 in LYR days, placing it in the 1915 batch of vehicles built at Horwich. Here we see the window of the somewhat cramped driver's compartment of an original third class motor car. The narrow platform canopy extended for some distance from the ELR headquarters. In the distance, work appears to be in progress in the rebuilding of the booking office, hall and footbridge following the fire of 1947. *H.C.Casserley.***

rooms, rest rooms, WCs, urinals, parcel office, telegraph office, guards' room, stores, porters room and station master's office.

The down platform made do with much less, although there was more than adequate provision for the call of nature, plus segregated waiting rooms and an inspector's office.

One of the major modifications carried out by the LYR occurred in 1916 in preparation for the Manchester-Bury electrification scheme. Despite the high emphasis on war casualties, the *Radcliffe Guardian* of 19th February 1916 found space to inform its readers that,

> "With the advent of electrification of the Manchester to Bury railway, Bolton Street station is to become a 'closed' station. Workmen are at present engaged on constructing an office on the landing leading from the entrance gangway to the two platforms, and it is there, we understand, where the barriers will be erected. Two female collectors commenced duty on Monday. The date of opening for traffic of the electric system has not been fixed but we also understand that the 'closed' arrangement may come into operation before then if everything is ready to do so". [Electric trains first ran on 16th April 1916]

In order to supply water to the station, the LYR had at some time built an elevated water tank overlooking the Down platform on land supported by the retaining wall. The tank stored water for a number of water columns which supplied water to steam locomotives passing through or working at the station.

In the early post-war years, the London Midland & Scottish Railway announced that Bolton Street station should undergo a lengthy rebuilding programme. The station had probably changed very little from the LYR days described above. However, the LMS plans were forestalled on 14th May 1947 when in the early morning a fire destroyed the street-level booking hall and roofed footbridge. After some delay, Bury Town Council asked British Railways to revitalise the station and by 1950, the station entrance, booking hall and footbridge were remodelled in brick and concrete. In the meantime the old ELR headquarters building became temporary station offices and access to the platforms was via this building onto platform 2. The new station frontage was opened on 30th June 1952 and remains today as the gateway to the East Lancashire Preserved Railway.

From Buckley Wells, Bolton Street station was approached by three running lines: Down slow, which served platform 4; Down fast, which served platform 3; and Up main which served platform 2. An unusual signalling arrangement prevailed on the Down slow line through the station which was bi-directional so that electric trains could move in both directions, meet each other and couple up if desired, all under strict control of Bury North and South signal boxes. To enable the passage of trains from Holcombe Brook to travel 'wrong line' into platforms 3 and 4, a set of fixed home signals were set at danger so that all movements from north to south were controlled by calling-on arms mounted under them. These signals were located in front of Bury North box. There were also two signals mounted on a bracket affixed to the stone retaining wall overlooking the line which served platform 4. These were arranged back to back, and close together, their function being to control the movement of trains along platform 4 from either direction, under 'calling-on regulations' at a maximum speed of 6 m.p.h., with motormen "prepared to stop short of any obstruction". A two-car Holcombe Brook train could just be admitted at the north end, whilst a five-car electric train from Manchester could fit at the southern end. Nearby, two similar signals were slung under the platform canopy and controlled train movements along the Down line adjacent to platform 3. Evidence of the wall-mounted signal can still be seen.

Sometime in the 1930s, the LMS installed colour searchlight signals at the southern approach to the station. A set of these were mounted on a right-hand bracket and extended over the Down slow and Down fast lines, opposite Angle Sidings. The colour lights were reputed to be American in concept, each one of the four able to show red, yellow

and green depending on the controlling hand of the signalman in Bury South box. A colour light signal of more modern design, was positioned near to the end of the Down platform, the main signal lights mounted on a straight post and showing two aspects: yellow (top) and red (bottom), both controlled by Bury South box. A subsidiary signal on the post was bracketed to the right. Both signals controlled departures from the south end of the station, the main aspects for the Up line, the subsidiary signal for wrong-line working in the Up direction along the Down slow line. Such signalling arrangements were confined to these two examples, no other location at or near Bolton Street receiving similar treatment.

On the west side of the station, overlooking the northern end of the Down platform, stood the Picture Theatre House, known locally as the Castle Picture House before it became the Bury Palais in 1939. Some readers might remember those days with nostalgia as they sat watching a black and white film, the sound drowned for a few moments by the passing of steam or electric trains in the station. How the vibrations and noise affected the dancing in Palais days has not been recorded!

Knowsley Street Station (also known as Low Level due to its position on a route which passed beneath the Clifton Jct to Rawtenstall line) - Some idea of the Bury Station is revealed in official plans drawn up by the Liverpool & Bury Railway Company in 1845. In these very early days, the Bury station was situated on the south side of John Street bridge (built 1848), a short cul-de-sac which was later extended by Bury Town Council to join Manchester Road at Buckley Wells, then being renamed Knowsley Street. The tenancy plan shows that Bury Station consisted of two platforms, one served by an up (Manchester) line and a down (Bolton) line. Attached to the Up platform was a small booking office which could be reached from John Street by a sloping path, accompanied by a stone wall which mounted a high stone retaining wall encompassing the station yard. The Down platform was an island type, since it was passed on the southern side by two goods only lines which branched off the main lines east of the station. A photograph of the station shows that the platforms were of low height and the only way of changing platforms was by dint of crossing the main lines.

By July 1847, the station was in the hands of the LYR. Company Executive Minutes of 8th March 1848 indicate that changes were afoot at the station: a Mr G.Thomson was contracted to build a wooden station house costing a total of £240.

Between the years 1866 and 1888, Bury station received the official title of Market Place and it was during this time of gradual expansion that the station was the scene of a serious accident. This occurred in 1871, and was reported in the *Middleton Albion* on the 14th October of that year:

> "At an early hour on Tuesday morning, a somewhat serious accident occurred at Knowsley Street station, Bury, on the Lancashire and Yorkshire Railway, whereby one poor fellow lost his life. It appears that a goods train from Liverpool to Oldham, which arrived here at 4.15 a.m., was standing on the proper metals, and has passed the points, with the exception of four wagons, when a goods train from Preston to Oldham came dashing along the East Lancashire line at such a speed as to prevent its driver pulling up in time to prevent a collision".

Greasy rails and a miscalculation of speed by the Preston-Oldham driver caused the smashing up of four wagons and the death of the stoker of the other goods train. Significantly, the reporter of this accident referred to the station as 'Knowsley Street', despite the official title of Market Place.

The gradual expansion of the station was in a piecemeal fashion. Buildings were grafted on in an apparently haphazard way; there were three different stages of platform canopies erected, the earliest being a ridge

Knowsley Street station staff and friends in LYR days. Each man and boy knew his place in the pecking order, the personnel presided over by the Station Master, a man respected and of some importance in the town, down to the lowly telegraph boy, seen here seated on a wad of sacking. There was pride in working for the railway, the free uniform worn as a mantle of service to the Company. Everybody bar one, probably the booking clerk, wears headress of one kind or another. Other features worthy of note include the bold LYR station signs, the modern gas lamp, the standard pattern valence and the signal gantry, spanning all four roads, supporting the brace of Down, lower quadrant signals. *Bury Central Library.*

and furrow design which was later extended over the up platform by a more prosaic gabled variety. The following extracts give some idea as to the method of expansion adopted by the LYR:- *Contract advert for footbridge and waiting rooms:* let to J.Kirkbride for £1,950, November 1893. *Further roof alterations, staircase and raising of platforms:* Contract awarded to Charles Brierley for £1,912 10s 1d, 22nd April 1886. *Additional platform roofing:* let to R. Neill for £2,006, 26th April 1899.

Turn of the century plans of the LYR system reveal that in 1891 widening had taken place so that four roads passed through the station between the Up (Castleton direction) and Down platforms, the through lines being in the middle. The Up platform was the longer (230 yds), extending eastwards, and having on its rear side a bay adjacent to the goods shed. This platform possessed the main amenities ranging from a booking office, waiting rooms, left luggage office, parcels office and WCs. Access could be made from Knowsley Street via a brick entrance building which led to a booking hall and covered footbridge down a staircase. Alternatively, a covered inclined L-shaped gangway led from Knowsley Street and entered the booking hall, this being most suitable for wheeled conveyances. The Down platform (160 yards long) could be reached by the footbridge and by a sloping path from Knowsley Street. Facilities here were adequate, consisting of a ticket collectors cab, waiting rooms, W.H.Smith bookstall, WCs and urinals.

It was the LYR footbridge, which had been erected about 1893/4, which collapsed under the weight of football supporters queuing for their train home on 19th January 1952. Despite only one fatality, the infamous demise of bridge No.18 will be forever associated with Knowsley Street station.

The only colour-light signals at Knowsley Street station stood over the Down line platform, the four aspects controlling the lines to Bolton, with two 'feathers' for Bolton Street station.

It was from the Down side platform, near the footbridge, that the 'hump' could be seen. This was an abrupt change in gradient of the Bolton to Rochdale line where it dipped below the bridge carrying the 'lecky' line to Bolton Street Station, officially known as "Bury Hollow". It

was at Bury Hollow that special instructions were issued to engine crews, signalmen and guards. The following are extracts from the *1931 LMS Sectional Appendix*:

"The driver of a freight train on approaching Bury Hollow on the Down line must keep on steam until the rear brake van is at the bottom of the Hollow, when he must gradually shut off steam, and nor resume it again until he feels the couplings tight and has received a signal from the guard to proceed. On approaching the Hollow on the Up line, he must keep on steam until arrival of the engine at Bury West box, where steam must be shut off and the tender brake applied cautiously until the rear brake van has arrived opposite the same box, or until the driver feels that the couplings of the train are tight....."

A further brief instruction read as follows: "Double heading of loaded coal trains through Bury Hollow is prohibited"

The possibility of freight trains breaking loose in Bury Hollow was also considered in those days of loose-coupled wagons: "Guards of trains which have broken loose must pull over the break-loose lever fixed on the Down side of the main line near Bury Hollow. This will be indicated in Bury (Knowsley Street) west box by a disc and the ringing of a bell. The guard must immediately afterwards telephone to the signalman at Bury West and Gas Sidings boxes and inform them what has occurred by using the telephone fixed in a hut near to the break-loose lever....."

Michael Blakemore in an article "Railways Through Bury" in the *Railway Magazine* February 1973, gives a nostalgic description of the station after Knowsley Street had closed on 5th October 1970:

"Unmourned by the majority of Philistines, those flaring gas lamps, the gloomy plank-covered passages and the unmistakable odour of old railway station will be missed by the few who appreciate such delicacies. It suffered from the disadvantage of being separated from the town centre and the buses by a long and exposed walk, and this, no doubt, contributed to its ultimate unpopularity."

Though unloved, Knowsley Street station held for many people memories of holiday and day excursions during the 1950s. The following is a selection of excursions which left the station between 7th July and 21st July 1956, the dates for Bury, Ramsbottom and Radcliffe annual holidays.

Schedule No.	To	Departs
41	Lytham, St Annes, Squires Gate, Blackpool	8.15am
42	Lytham, St Annes, Squires Gate, Blackpool	4.52pm
44	Blackpool North	7.46pm
202	Bridlington, Filey, Scarborough	10.07am
174	Carnforth, Oxenholme, Kendal, Windermere, Penrith, Keswick; Change at Bolton	10.19am

Bury East Fork - The two stations were connected by Bury East Fork which was opened for traffic on the 20th November 1848. This link permitted southbound trains on the ELR line to gain access to the Bolton-Rochdale line (and vice versa) and thence to Rochdale and Manchester. The Fork was, in the words of Eric Mason, 'a steeply graded and curved connection' and served the system in Bury until shortly before its demise, as a single track along which coal trains from Yorkshire headed for the Rawtenstall Coal Concentration plant and returned with empties.

Pedestrians could also communicate between the stations on foot by means of a footpath which closely followed the East Fork until the latter's junction with the EL line at Bury South Junction (hitherto known as East Lancashire Junction). From here, the path diverged from the railway, passed under Tenterden Street bridge and entered Bolton Street station yard, closely following the stone revetment. The footpath closed on safety grounds about 1950.

The Bury Loop. (also known as the Bury Connecting Line) - The Loop was a longer, less steeply graded and less tightly curved connection between the Rochdale-Bolton line, at Bury Loop Junction, and the Manchester-Bury line at Loco Junction. Its purpose was to enable the heavy goods traffic from Yorkshire and elsewhere to reach Manchester Docks without the need to reverse at Windsor Bridge Junction. Excursion traffic also used the Loop, plus light engines running on and off shed at Buckley Wells. The advantages of the Loop was appreciated by the LYR and witnessed its authorisation by an Act dated 3rd July 1891, placing the contract in the hands of Thomas Wrigley, whose tender of £30,866 was found acceptable. A letter to the B.O.T. in November 1898 included plans and sections, the following being the bulk of the details furnished by the LYR:

> BURY CONNECTING LINE "This consists of a new railway joining the Manchester and Bury Railway with the Bury and Rochdale Railway. Width of formation level - 30 feet. Gauge - 4' 8½". Two running roads (Up and Down) with six feet between. In connection with the new railway, certain alterations have been carried out to the Permanent Way of the Bury and Rochdale line....Which was forwarded to the Board of Trade on October 15th 1898. The rails are steel, weighing 86 lbs per lineal yard. Length of each rail 30 feet. Weight of chairs 56 lbs each. These are fastened to sleepers by two treenails (a pin of hardwood) and two spikes. The joints of the rails are fastened with fishplates and lock nuts. The sleepers are Baltic Timber creosoted, 9 feet long, 10" x 5" and laid transversely, and the distance from centre to centre is 2' 9½" except at joints where it is two feet. The ballast consists of hand-packed pitching and cinders. The fencing consists of oak posts with 5 rails and two prick posts to each length of 10 feet, and brick and stone walls and sleepers." W.Worthington 23rd November 1898.

Elsewhere in the documentation, mention is made of the civil engineering involved for the Loop to pass under two main roads leading out of Bury:

> "There is no Tunnel but the space between Manchester Old Road and Manchester New Road bridges has been arched over at the request of the Corporation. This makes the total length of the covered way, including the two bridges, of 70 yards."

Inevitably, the construction of the loop through a built-up area caused some problems to existing properties. In the area of the 'Tunnel', some property had to be demolished whilst Back Manchester Old Road was 'stopped', its original passage into Baron Street severed. These consequences had been planned for, but others were unexpected. A report in

Stanier 'Black 5' 45208 draws a short rake of wagons along the Bury Loop towards Bury Loop Junction on 6th October 1965. Knowsley Street station is hidden by the loco exhaust, but other elements of the Knowsley Street area infrastructure can be seen including several water columns of LYR origin, a fogman's hut, and a fully-operational goods shed. The view is from Market Street bridge. *R.J.Farrell.*

the *Bury Times* (sometime during 1898) referred to the danger to a public amenity close to the construction site near the 70 yards tunnel:

> "The new drinking fountain on Manchester Road, costing £600 was erected at Buckley Wells. The new fountain was erected 20 months before the construction of the Bury Loop line between the ELR line and Knowsley Street station. The result was that while demolition of the old property at the junction of the roads was in progress, and during the subsequent tunnelling operations in the vicinity, the fountain, which was completed on 5th October 1897 had to be boxed in, in order to protect it from injury".

On completion, the Bury Loop Line was inspected by the B.O.T and passed for passenger traffic on the 11th July 1899.

Handling Freight - The number of goods handling facilities in Bury in the early years of the 20th century included both LYR and privately owned yards and sidings. The following is an alphabetical list of sidings functioning in the town as printed in the *Railway Clearing House Handbook* for 1904:

Angle Sidings (adjacent to Bolton Street Station).
Ashworth's Siding (Arthur Ashworth's Chemical Works).
Atherton's Siding (Atherton's Timber Yard at Buckley Wells).
Buckley Wells Siding.
Bury Corporation Siding (Tottington Jct).
Bury Corporation Electricity Siding. (Tottington Jct).
Bury Gas Siding.
Bury Saw Mill Siding (later New Bury Saw Mill) (Tottington Jct).
Fernhill Siding (Tottington Jct).
Locomotive Siding (Buckley Wells).
Paper Co.Siding (Gigg).
Park Siding (Tottington Jct).
Peel Mill Siding (Tottington Jct).
Pilot Mill Siding (Gigg).
Railway Pit Siding.
Shell Mex Siding.
Smith's Siding (Buckley Wells).
Wigan Coal & Iron Siding (Buckley Wells).

By 1925, two years into the LMS period, the number had been reduced to fifteen, with some of the 1904 facilities still extant:

Ashworth's (Fernhill Sidings).
Atherton's Siding.
Buckley Wells Sidings.
New Bury Saw Mill Sidings.
Bury Corporation Electricity Sidings.
Bury Corporation Gasworks Sidings.
Knowsley St. Sidings.
LMS Railway Sidings (Angle Sidings).
Paper Mill Sidings.
Peel Mill Sidings.
Permanent Way Sidings.
Pilot Mill Siding.
Shell Mex Sidings.
Wigan Coal and Iron Siding.

In terms of size alone, Knowsley Street Sidings covered the biggest area. In its heyday it was known by railway employees and the general public as "The L and Y" to distinguish it from those yards and sidings closely tied to the ELR. The map of 1845 shows the layout of the yard and reveals that there were three buildings, two warehouses and a cotton shed. A lengthy and narrow warehouse nearest the station had rail access as did the other two buildings. By dint of wagon turntables a number of sidings and tracks splayed out in different directions so allowing access to all the buildings by wagon. This layout persisted into

LYR days and formed the basis of what could be seen well into BR days. A large brick cotton warehouse replaced the earlier narrow shed the contract let to J. Byron for £5,448, the building having a 40 ton electric overhead travelling crane. The warehouse was completed about 1912. The old cotton shed in LYR days was divided up into different areas, storage, stores, office etc, whilst buildings outside provided stables mess room, blacksmith's shop and an office for Joseph Nall the LYR's haulage agent. A smaller goods shed had three floors and was utilised for general merchandise.

Along the rear of the yard was a loading platform and a cattle wagon siding and pens which provided temporary accommodation to arriving cattle before being herded a short distance to Bury Corporation Abattoir just off Knowsley Street. Up to the Second World War, transport around the town relied heavily on horsepower hence the large amount of space devoted to stabling, storage of hay and peat moss bedding, manure pits and smithy's shop for the maintenance of carts, wheels and axles. A heavy cart demanded great strength from a single horse as it plodded up the goods yard incline leading to Knowsley Street. A particularly heavy load demanded the use of a chain horse which would be positioned in front of the first horse.

Knowsley Street yard stretched eastwards as far as Heywood Street South, Market Street Bridge spanning the widening yard by a set of four arches.

In contrast, Castlecroft yard occupied a small area to the north of Bolton Street, hemmed in by the main running lines, Tanpits Road and Castlecroft Road. The ELR, on deciding that the conveyance of freight was a viable proposition, built a stone warehouse in 1848, unusual because its front doors faced almost 90 degrees to the main railway. A set of seven sidings, two of which ran into the warehouse, trailed back from a loop siding, each one of the seven having hardly enough space to straighten before ending at buffer stops. The warehouse housed four wooden stages on which were mounted various rooms for general offices and a mess. Outer buildings were few in number and included a store room, stables, and mess rooms, all these located at the rear of the yard. Access to the yard was from Castle Croft Road.

Fred Campbell worked at Castlecroft Goods during the 1920s and his description of that line reveals the immense amount of activity which this small yard generated in association with the town's major industries:

> "There was plenty of weighing to do, for lorries and carts passed in and out all day long with a wide variety of goods. They brought cow hides for Harvey's Tannery, which eventually came back as leather; sheep skins for Bury Wool Company (the wool came back after processing); cotton for the mills at Daisyfield; steel billets and blooms for Webbs, which came back as forgings; waste for Spencer and Curedale, and Frank Rixon at Bury Ground; paper from Crompton's and round timber for Wormald's and Fulton's"

Directly opposite Castlecroft yard, occupying an area of land between Peel Tannery and Castle Armoury lay School Brow Coal Sidings. This yard consisted of three sidings which curved off an Up loop siding, and just enough space left over for a coal stacking ground and a 5 ton crane. Access to the yard was by a gated entrance on School Brow.

Angle Sidings lay to the south of Bolton Street station, occupying an area of land bordered by East Fork, Bury Loop and the main running lines. Rail access was made to the three short sidings from the Down line of East Fork, branching off immediately before Bury South Junction, whilst a southern access (or exit) was available from behind Bury South Signal box (LYR brick 1910) by a line running under the Belle Vue Terrace Footbridge and over the Bolton to Rochdale line.

The Buckley Wells Complex - Reference to an early O.S. map of Bury, surveyed in 1844 and published 1851, shows the existence of an 'engine house' situated adjacent to the main line and to the south of

Coal Pit Lane at Buckley Wells. Captain Tucker's O.S. map of 1846/7 also shows the same structure, thought to be a small timber 'engine shed' which had been erected by the ELR. This building has been interpreted as having been the ELR's locomotive works and Company Board Minutes make references to the effect that the facility was unsatisfactory for the Company's requirements. Undaunted by the lean years following the collapse of the money market of 1846, the ELR organised a competition in which new designs for a more substantial works would be encouraged. Prizes were offered, as the following extract from the *Manchester Examiner* of 27th February 1847 shows:

> "The East Lancashire Railway are prepared to give a premium
> of £100 for the best and £50 for the second best plan and design
> of the buildings necessary for the making and repairing of the
> locomotive engines and carriages of the Company, such plans
> to be accompanied by full and explanatory details."

Financial insecurity resulted in the abandonment of the scheme and the designs, if ever they were submitted, were shelved and forgotten. Whilst the ELR expanded its network in Lancashire, the facilities at Buckley Wells developed by accretion, haphazardly, and continued to remain inadequate for the Company's requirements.

By April 1853, little had been done to improve matters, and it fell to J.S.Perring, the ELR engineer, to draw up plans for a permanent locomotive, carriage and wagon works. No action was taken until 1855. On 20th March, Perring submitted his outline plans to the ELR Directors who then asked for details, specifications and cost estimates for the locomotive works. By September 1855, land had been purchased (13,645 sq yards, bought in August 1855 at 2/6d per acre) and the *Manchester Guardian* of 22nd September 1855 carried a contract advert when the ELR invited tenders for the erection of locomotive workshops, comprising the erecting of machines, boiler-maker's shop, smithy, brass foundry, offices, stores and engine house. The tender of James Hill for £6,600 was accepted. Buckley Wells locomotive works opened during the summer of 1856 and was designed and built to stable and repair locomotives, although the rebuilding of locomotives, especially the bank of ELR 2-2-2s which were converted to a 2-4-0 wheel arrangement. The works had complete autonomy after the takeover of the ELR by the LYR in 1859, and this persisted until the death of the work's superintendent Sylvester Lees on 22nd March 1865.

During the 1860s, the locomotive works was extended and altered to suit the needs of the LYR. Further alteration took place in the 1870's with the construction of the attached engine shed on the west side, a building familiar to many, completed in 1876 and closed in April 1965. With the near completion of Horwich Works in January 1888, locomotive repair was transferred there from Buckley Wells leaving the derelict building ideally suited to carriage repair and maintenance. The *Railway Times* of 7th January 1888 carried the terse statement: "The workshops at Bury were closed at the end of 1887 when Horwich works was opened."

The O.S. plan of 1893 shows the remodelled works sandwiched between the 1875 engine shed and a wagons works to the east. In 1914/15 the carriage works changed its function once again and became an electric car depot serving stock in use on the Manchester-Bury line. The *Manchester Guardian* of 9th March 1913 carried a LYR contract advert which invited tenders for the conversion of the carriage shed at Bury into a carriage repair shop. This remained its function until September 1991.

The ex-locomotive works, ex-carriage shop, ex-electric car depot is still extant and is now Grade 2 listed. Some 600 feet long, twin bayed and of modular design (suitable for extension), the building was brick-built, its slated roof laid on stout wooden trusses supported by hollow iron columns which permitted drainage. The shed originally housed five roads, and after 1915/16 the approach roads were provided with an electrified third rail.

At the Coal Pit Lane end, two-storey brick offices had been built in the

1860's: The *Manchester Guardian* of 26th October 1861, carried the LYR contract advert inviting tenders "for the erection of offices at the locomotive shops at Buckley Wells".

The 1937 O.S. plan shows both the 'engine shed' and 'carriage shed', the third LYR component, the wagon works having been removed leaving the area it occupied as a coal yard with seven sidings.

Between 1846 and 1870, the ELR carriage and wagon superintendency was held by James Newall, who, at some time during his career, must have presided over the Buckley Wells complex. He was also director of the Lancashire and Yorkshire Wagon Company at Heywood (with Sylvester Lees) from 1857 and his interest in mechanical engineering gave rise to the invention of a braking system, known as Newall's Continuous Brake. This was applied to wagons and carriages and tested on the ELR such that between 15th September and 7th November 1853, an experimental train ran 5,874 miles without mishap.

On 22nd October 1853, a gathering of forty engineers from various railway companies congregated at Bury to witness a series of tests which were carried out on the Baxendale Bank near Accrington. Further tests also occurred between Southport and Liverpool and on the 1 in 27 Werneth Incline between Middleton Junction and Werneth Station. On both occasions, Newall's braking system was compared to that of Charles Fay (LYR) system. Newall died on 21st August 1870 after almost 30 years of service to the ELR and LYR.

Bury Engine Shed - Part of the Buckley Wells complex of the 1840s was the primitive engine shed-cum-locomotive works built by the ELR for its engines plying between Manchester, Bury and Rawstenstall. The timber structure stood alongside the up main line and after the building of the new locomotive works in 1855/56, the old engine shed and the new works appeared on an early map of 1857 which had been deposited for Parliamentary approval by the Bury Gas Light and Coke Co.Ltd. By 1863, a more detailed plan showed both buildings and the network of railway tracks serving the 'engine shed' and the "Lancashire & Yorkshire Railway Locomotive Department". At this stage, the two buildings were separate, the latter building connected by turntable to a siding linking Buckley Wells Coal Sidings by crossing Coal Pit Lane. The engine shed was then served by five roads.

By 1872, the engine shed was in a dilapidated condition and yet, there followed years of procrastination by the LYR ever mindful of outlaying money. By 1874, a decision was finally made to replace the existing shed; estimates were obtained for a modern building in a variety of styles, of stone, brick and timber, the first the most expensive, the last, the cheapest. Further indecision followed, as reflected in the following minute taken from the LYR Board Minutes of 26th May 1875:

> "Mr. Thomson pointed out that to build the new engine shed at
> Bury in stone will not merely cost £150 more than if it were in
> brick, but it will also take longer. For many reasons brick is
> preferable to stone for this particular purpose, so he will move
> the use of brick notwithstanding the previous Board resolution."

The following month it was finally decided to construct a straight shed in brick at a cost of £7,300, the contract awarded to William Dransfield. It opened some twelve months later. The O.S. plan of 1893 shows the 1876, 8-road shed adjoining the west elevation of the carriage works, the rear of the engine shed flanking Coal Pit Lane. The shed yard in 1893 possessed a 50 ft turntable and a standard LYR 'tank-over' coal hole. The 1938 plan shows that the 1893 infrastructure remained the same except for the addition of a sand-drying plant located near the front of the electric car works.

During the LYR period, Bury shed was identified by the code 20 and served the Bury area by accommodating and maintaining Barton Wright and Aspinall 0-6-0 goods engines, having in the region of 50 locomotives in the mid-1920s. The locomotive allocation on the 31st December 1921 (the last day before the L&Y became part of the L&NWR)

numbered seventy one and was as follows:-

Class 5 **2-4-2T** 24, 104, 349, 707, 1012, 1333.
Class 21 **0-4-0ST** 298, 402, 729.
Class 23 **0-6-0ST** 143, 144, 174, 250, 256, 268, 311, 538, 544, 561, 615, 751, 753, 756, 757, 787, 796, 801, 858, 861.
Class 25 **0-6-0** 930, 938, 939.
Class 26 **2-6-2T** 1444, 1450.
Class 27 **0-6-0** 30, 44, 73, 77, 92, 103, 130, 213, 320, 333, 372, 427, 473, 478, 685, 834, 875, 1058, 1065, 1073, 1128, 1145, 1188, 1193, 1233, 1241, 1249, 1276.
Class 28 **0-6-0** 52, 219, 342, 474, 521, 642, 1123, 1247.

The first proper LMS shed coding was C20, the shed being in what became the Central Division of that company, then in 1935 it became 26D when the LMS introduced a 'Concentration scheme' for its motive power depots. Bury became a 'garage shed' under the parent shed Newton Heath, 26A. In 1963 it was recoded to 9M.

A gradual decline in allocation set in after the Second World War, the number of locomotives in 1945 being:-
LMS 7F 0-8-0 (7); ex LYR 2P 2-4-2T (5); ex LYR 2F 0-6-0st (7); ex LYR 3F 0-6-0 (12), making a total of 31 locomotives.

The allocation on the last day of the LMS (31/12/47) had risen slightly to 39 but was still virtually half that of L&Y days:-

L&Y Class 2F **0-6-0ST** 11338, 11419,11481, 11486, 11487, 11489, 11504.
L&Y Class 2P **2-4-2T** 10823, 10872, 10875, 10892.
LMS Class 4P **2-6-4T** 2473, 2474, 2476, 2629.
L&Y Class 3F **0-6-0** 12129, 12139, 12159, 12164, 12165, 12245, 12246, 12382, 12455, 12554, 12579, 12580, 12581, 12608, 12615.
LMS Class 7F **0-8-0** 9557, 9590, 9591, 9594, 9665, 9666, 9667.
LMS Class 8F **2-8-0** 8768, 8769.

This allocation can be compared with that of 1959 (after the Bacup line had been dieselised) when, it will be noted, the ex-Ministry of Supply WD 2-8-0s had replaced the former LMS 0-8-0 and 2-8-0s for most of the heavy freight workings. Some of the old Lanky 0-6-0s lingered on doing sterling work on virtually any job entrusted to them - they were workhorses and their longevity is testimony to that fact:-
LMS 5MT 2-6-0 (6); LMS 4P 2-6-4T (4); L&Y 3F 0-6-0 (4); LMS 3F 0-6-0T (1); LMS 2MT 2-6-0 (5); WD 2-8-0 (11) *Total 31*.

Towards the end of the steam era in April 1965, an allocation of 20 locomotives was left, these eventually transferred to other sheds or sent for scrapping, their useful life, on the eve of diesel power, at an end. The depot from 1967 was utilised as a storage place for GEC-built AL4 later Class 84 Bo-Bo electric locomotives [Nos E3036, E3038, E3041, E3042, E3044 and E3045] plus a number of AL3s - Class 83, all of which had unreliable mercury-arc rectifiers and were marked down for withdrawal. Since there was no accommodation at Longsight shed, the electrics were hauled to Bury by 8F 2-8-0 No.48025, probably one of the last jobs it did. Other extraneous locomotives stored at ex-9M were 'Jubilee' No.45596 BAHAMAS (destined for preservation), electric locomotives (ex Manchester - Sheffield line) E26000 TOMMY the pioneer LNER Bo-Bo EM1 and all seven of the larger Class EM2 Co-Co locomotives, E27000 to E27006, the latter class eventually purchased by Dutch Railways for whom they gave many more years of service.

Buckley Wells Crossing occurred where Coal Pit Lane crossed the railway on the level. This was controlled by Buckley Wells Level Crossing box which was opened on 22nd January 1949 as a replacement for an LYR box at the same location from 1872, until its closure when the new box came into use. The new box had been built in the space behind the old box, then moved forward on rails when the latter had been demolished. Nearby were Buckley Wells Coal Sidings occupying an area of land between the main running lines and rows of terraced houses between Belle Vue Terrace and Baron Street. In 1863, these sidings comprised six roads four of which were short in length, another crossing Coal Pit Lane and then running parallel to the locomotive works. A sixth siding ran alongside a loading platform adjacent to the aforementioned houses. Access was from Baron Street, the entrance having a weighing machine and office. The 1893 maps shows an additional siding, the through-siding now truncated and giving way to the wagon works offices. By 1937, the number of sidings had reached ten, and were 'paired' rather than laid as individual roads as previously. Rail access was from a continuation of a looped siding from Angle Sidings, the so-called 'Coal Road', which passed over the Bolton-Rochdale line and under Belle Vue Terrace footbridge.

(below) **Bury steam shed, 8th February 1964. Even by this date, 9M (26D) was well-occupied by locos in steam; 46412, 42700, and three other unidentified Ivatt Class 2s.** *R.J.Farrell.*

13

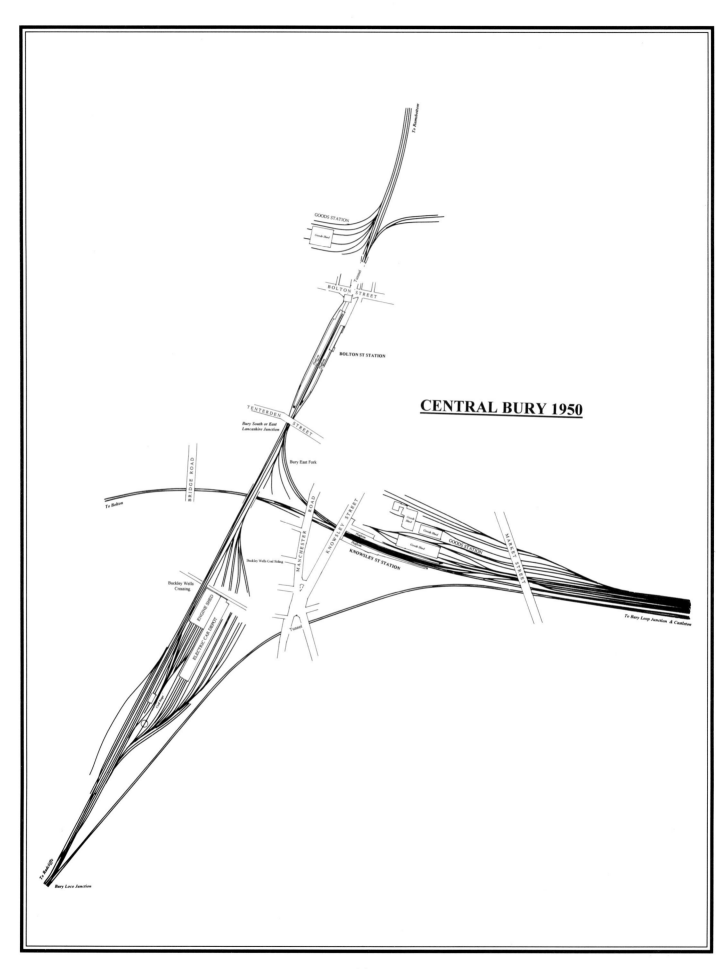

CENTRAL BURY 1950

(above) Beneath the canopy, Bolton Street station frontage. Under Statutory Rules and Orders No.2078, amalgamation of the LYR and LNWR had been effected from January 1921. Not surprisingly, the latter company deemed it necessary to mark the amalgamation at the station by erecting this indicator board, incorporating the advertising centre piece. As No.D22, the wooden construction measured 13ft 10ins x 12ft 10ins and was erected on 19th August 1922. *Manchester Loco. Society.*

(right) A general view of Bolton Street station taken from Tenterden Street bridge, 14th August 1953. Four sets of ex-LYR electric units occupy the station. A five-car train led by M28515 (LYR 3517) begins to leave platform 3 for Manchester. Note the off shunting signal (No.42) giving a clear road on the Up main out of the station. *F.W.Shuttleworth.*

Bolton Street station at 11a.m. on a wet 17th October 1959. Three types of rail transport are shown in this view: an ex-LYR, five-car train occupies platform 4; a Metro-Cam d.m.u. awaits departure from platform 3: stabled in bay platform 1 are a pair of Wolverton built e.m.u.s newly in service in their green livery. Note the use of an oil lamp at the front of the LYR unit (a somewhat incongruous utility), and the high, sloped, retaining wall on the east side of the station. *A. J. Cocker.*

(left) Steps erected by the East Lancashire Railway providing access to Bolton Street station from Bank Street and the footpath which runs along the top of the retaining wall.

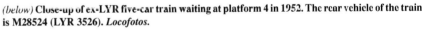

(below) Close-up of ex-LYR five-car train waiting at platform 4 in 1952. The rear vehicle of the train is M28524 (LYR 3526). *Locofotos.*

(above) **Bolton Street, 1952.** Two ex-LYR units have been stabled in the short electrified spur which trailed back from the Down slow line, near platform 4. The forward car is **M29210 (LYR 3512)**, a third class trailer of 1915 vintage. Notice the detail of the iron work on Tenterden Street bridge (dated 1848), the bridge being swept away in the town's new road system, Jubilee Way replacing the bridge, circa 1976. *Locofotos.*

(right) **Bolton Street station.** Wall-mounted signals above the Down line, adjacent to platform 4. To enable the station to cope more efficiently with terminating trains from Holcombe Brook and from Manchester, bi-directional signalling was brought into use on platforms 3 and 4 on Sunday 1st September 1918. To ensure safety, the signals for the Up (southbound) trains were controlled by both North and South signal boxes, and would not clear until both signalmen had pulled the appropriate levers. The nearer signal was worked by lever 24 in North box, and the signal behind it by lever 7 (North) and lever 25 (South). Both arms were originally lower quadrant, but by the time of the photograph, 1952, signal 7/25 had been renewed as upper quadrant. *Locofotos.*

(lower right) The same pair of signals looking south from the Down platform. Above the retaining wall, to the left, is an elevated L&Y standard pattern water tank erected to provide a pressured water supply for the station. *Locofotos.*

LANCASHIRE & YORKSHIRE RAILWAY
THE BUSINESS LINE

A quiet spell at Bolton Street, 27th March 1959. Platform 4 and 1 are occupied by ex-LYR electric stock shortly before their demise and removal from the scene. One could be forgiven for believing that the station saw only electric stock as not a whiff of smoke or steam is to be seen. *R. J. Farrell.*

Every self-respecting railway station possessed a W.H.Smith retail outlet, and Bolton Street station was no exception. The station entrance and booking hall were redeveloped following the fire of 1947, the W.H.Smith book and magazine stall opening on 30th June 1952. It was located on the right side of the booking hall on entry to the station from Bolton Street. The date of this view is 30th July 1952. *W.H.Smith Limited.*

A Cravens Two-car d.m.u. arrives at platform 3 from Manchester Victoria, 29th February 1964. A fine view of the sets of bracketed semaphores has been caught by the cameraman from his viewpoint from behind the retaining wall parapet on the east side of the station. The closest bracket controlled movements from bay platform 1: the tallest arms for departures to Radcliffe, the lower to Knowsley Street. The other bracket on platform 2 controlled departure to Radcliffe (tallest) and Knowsley Street. All the stop signals were worked from Bury South, the left-hand distants from Buckley Wells, the right-hand distants being fixed. *R. J. Farrell.*

Another Cravens d.m.u. departs from platform 2 en route to Manchester Victoria via Clifton Junction in the early 1960s. The 'off' semaphores, give a clear road ahead for the Up fast line out of the station. *R. J. Farrell.*

(above) **LYR official photograph of platforms 3 and 4, Bolton Street station showing the platform furniture, pendant gas lights and general sub-roof structure. The views to left and right have been deliberately faded to enhance the real focus of interest. The retaining wall to the right features many period adverts, although unfortunately not clear enough to decipher. *NRM (HOR F1810).***

(left) **Platforms 3 and 4 at Bolton Street station in April 1971 with a handful of passengers eagerly boarding a Manchester-bound e.m.u. The roof has undergone a transition at some time during the LMS period, whereby the equal pitched southlight roof, with glazed gables, shown in the view above, has been replaced by single pitch unglazed roof running along the length of the platform. Notice that the same cast-iron cloumns have been utilised. *Bury Central Library.***

(above) **Platforms 1 and 2 (No.1 being the old Up platform), Bolton Street, May 1971.** The East Lancashire Railway headquarters dominated the station: a Dickensian building with stone quoins, lintels, and arched windows and doors, its solid brick walls making the statement, 'built to last'. Note the tell-tale marks above the ground floor windows and doors, marks left after the removal of the platform canopy. Built to last it may have been, but the venerable old structure succumbed to the demolition man in 1972, leaving a vacant space and the wooden structures surmounting platforms 2 and 3. *Bury Central Library.*

(right) **The direct link between Bolton Street and Knowsley Street stations, Bury East Fork.** Ex-LMS 3F 47584 takes the sharply curved Up line, actually descending, towards Knowsley Street station with a single tank and brake van, 11th January 1960. *R. J. Farrell.*

This view of platforms 3 and 4 at Bolton Street station in March 1980 reveals the "cloistered" atmosphere beneath the LYR roof as passengers await the arrival of a train from Manchester. *Bury Central Library.*

A two-car e.m.u. awaits the time for departure from platform 3 at Bolton Street in March 1980. The station has been and is undergoing fundamental changes in its appearance: a car park now exists in place of the old ELR building and the Down main line has been cut at the end of the platform - note the buffer stop behind the train and the sign which reads "Trains Stop". *Bury Central Library.*

Bury East Lancs Tunnel looking towards Bolton Street station in the early 1970's. Although the line has been singled, the view illustrates what was left of the original infrastructure by that time. Bury North signal box was positioned in a recess in the retaining wall, and the castellated northern portal of the tunnel reminds us of its proximity to the site of Bury's medieval castle. *LYR Society Collection.*

Castlecroft Goods shed and yard in a state of change sometime in the 1970's. During 1972, the site was taken over the ELRPS for future use as the society museum. Here we see it littered with debris after its use by contractors involved in the construction of Peel Way, the town's northern bypass. *LYR Society Collection.*

(below) Knowsley Street station, 26th September 1953. Aspinall (Class 27) 3F, 0-6-0, No. 52245 pauses on the Down through road with a loose-coupled goods train. The first wagon is a 12 ton, 7-plank wagon, and still betrays its private ownership details which were painted on the side. Within twelve months 52245 had been withdrawn and had made the final journey to Horwich for scrapping. *F. W. Shuttleworth, LYR Collection.*

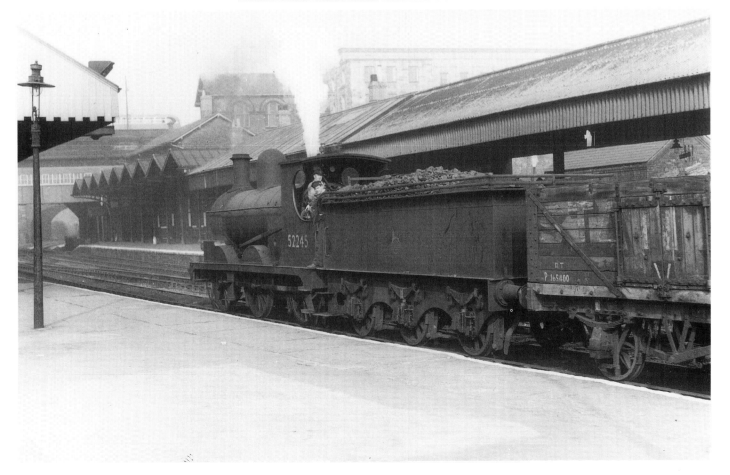

Hughes 5MT 2-6-0 No.42712, one of a class affectionately referred to as ''Crabs'', or, to the more technically minded, 'Moguls'. 42712, one of a 245 strong class introduced by the LMS with some built at Horwich, is drawing a rake of mineral wagons and a van, tender first through Knowsley Street Station, 2nd February 1963. The 1912 LYR brick goods warehouse forms an impressive backdrop to the train which has passed through the station on the Up through line. *R.J. Farrell.*

(below) The booking hall, Knowsley Street station. As at Bolton Street Station, the LNWR marked its influence by erecting an indicator board-cum-advertisement slot on 27th May 1922. The construction measured 16ft 7¼ ins. x 12ft 10½ ins. and was positioned perilously close to the foot of the stairs. *Manchester Locomotive Society.*

Knowsley Street, 2nd February 1963. A Cravens 2-car d.m.u. passes the 1912 goods warehouse. This 'distant' view provides an aspect of the eastern end of the station with Knowsley Street bridge in the background. Notice the Clock Tower which stands to this day in Tower Gardens at the junction of Knowsley Street and Manchester Road. *R. J. Farrell.*

Stanier Cl.5 4-6-0 No. 45206 leaves Knowsley Street station with the 9.5 a.m. Summer Saturdays only Liverpool Exchange to Scarborough train on 6th July 1963. Close examination of the photograph reveals that the Down platform is well-patronised: although private car ownership was increasing, the excursion to the coast and elsewhere was still made by train. A loading gauge can be seen suspended above the siding just inside one of the warehouse entrances. *R. J. Farrell.*

A Metro-Cammel d.m.u. forming a Bacup - Manchester via Heywood service leaves Knowsley Street on 27th June 1959, en route to Manchester Victoria. To the right of the d.m.u. is one of three gantries which supported the goods yard electric lighting system. *R. J. Farrell.*

The view eastwards from the Down platform at Knowsley Street as Cravens 2-car d.m.u., probably on the 11.40 a.m. Rochdale to Blackburn service arrives at the station on 2nd February 1963. Note the four arches of Market Street bridge which spanned the sidings, and the line of vans occupying the yard. *R. J. Farrell.*

With the Bury Loop Line behind the photographer, Stanier 3MT 2-6-2T No. 40142 hauls a "dead" Ivatt 4MT 2-6-0 No. 43121 en route to Horwich Locomotive Works via the down platform line. Note the long line of vans and the locomotive shunting in the yard. Date: 5th March 1960. *R. J. Farrell.*

Stanier Class 5 No. 45068 enters the Down platform with the 4.07 p.m. train to Bolton on the 24th April 1951. The scene is enhanced by the row of gas lamps and the typical LYR roof trusses silhouetted against the spring sky. *H. C. Casserley*.

'Crab' 42712 approaches Market Street bridge and Bury East Signal box. Note the fine set of signals mounted on a lattice gantry which spanned the Up reception sidings and the contrasting methods of obtaining water seen in the LYR parachute tank and the water column. At the foot of these are two overturned braziers and mounds of cinders from fires which prevented freezing up of the facilities in winter. *R. J. Farrell*.

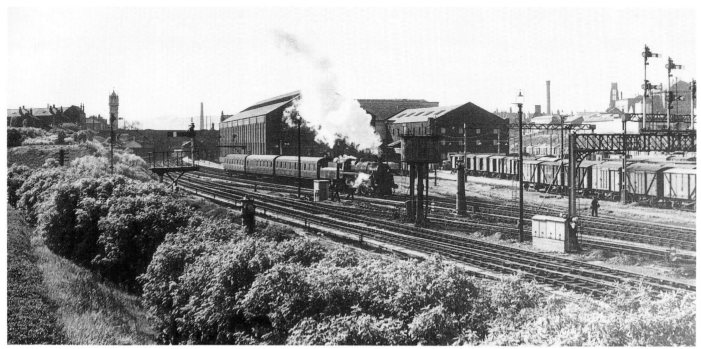

(above) A fine view of Knowsley Street station and goods yard fixed on film for posterity on 19th May 1965. BR Standard Class 4MT 4-6-0 No. 75047 draws a three-coach train away from the Up platform towards Broadfield and Heywood. It is a well-packed yard with vans indicating that even in the mid-1960s, a large (but nevertheless decreasing) volume of goods were conveyed by rail. *R. J. Farrell.*

(left) Knowsley Street station on a bright 30th July 1960. A Derby Class 108 diesel multiple unit with Cravens 2-car unit in the rear stand at the Up platform. Of the several similar views, this one clearly shows the colour light signals and route indicators over the Down platform and through lines. Clear too is the half-glazed footbridge which replaced the collapsed LYR version. With a magnifying glass, the 'hump' (Bury Hollow) can be seen dipping below the Clifton Jct - Rawtenstall line. *R. J. Farrell.*

LMS 3F 0-6-0T No. 47584 as busy as ever hauls a mixed load of freight along the Up line of the Bury Loop to Knowsley Street yard on 11th January 1960. Note the LYR water column situated next to the Down loop line. *R. J. Farrell.*

Equine activity at Knowsley Street station, 6th February 1934. Records of this official LMS photograph describe the event as "household removal to Torquay", evidently a wealthy personage possessing horses which needed transporting to the Torbay resort. While station staff and farmers struggle to ensconce the animals in special horse box wagons, an interested group looks on, made up of perhaps a mixture of railway officials and the owner. *National Railway Museum (Dy 18810).*

In addition to the transport of the stud, the household items had to be moved lock, stock and barrel to Torquay on the same day in 1934. The engine in charge of the first leg of the journey is ex-LNWR 'Super D' 0-8-0, LMS Class 7 No.9028. The bridge in view is Market Street bridge, beyond which is Knowsley Street station. *National Railway Museum (DY18812)*

Derby built Class 108 d.m.u. M50945 leads the way out of Knowsley Street with other, unidentified, diesel multiple units to the rear in the early 1960's. A mixed freight train approaches the station on the Down through line, hauled by a 'WD' which partially hides the Clock Tower with its blow-off steam. *R.J.Farrell.*

(below) Knowsley Street, 5th July 1968. A holiday special to Newquay, Cornwall leaves the station hauled by Rose Grove Class 5 No. 45156 AYRSHIRE YEOMANRY. The train is believed to have worked through to Stockport on the first leg of its long journey south, and was the last BR steam passenger train at Bury other than rail tours. *R.J.Farrell.*

30

Knowsley Street station frontage circa 1969. Never an inspiring place, at least from street level, but the ELR and later LYR never did go 'over the top' with station architecture, function rather than flair winning the day. All that remains today is the newspaper/sweet shop, still selling the same . *Bury Central Library.*

(below) Knowsley Street bereft of its awnings and on-the-road to demolition during its last week of operation in October 1970. Pupils from Bury Grammar School form the bulk of the payload on the 16.17 dmu service to Rochdale. Look carefully, you may be there and about to board the homeward-bound train! *M. Blakemore Collection.*

An interesting view of Knowsley Street goods yard in 1967, the cameraman standing on Market Street bridge to take his photograph. Although the station seems quiet, there is some activity in the yard: a mobile crane is at work in front of the 1912 goods shed, whilst a trailer is being loaded/unloaded alongside a line of vans. Other yard features of interest include the gantries, much like electrification catenary, used to suspend the lighting cables, the sheeted 'con-flat' container, the yard-staff huts and the Morris Minor parked in front of the mobile crane. *Bury Central Library.*

By the Summer of 1970, Knowsley Street station was slowly being taken apart as this view shows. The dismantling of the Up platform canopy was already underway, leaving the roof supports and columns to be dismantled. The Down platform has already suffered the indignity of being partially demolished leaving yawning gaps and semi-dereliction. An engineer's train stands or slowly moves through the station on the Down platform line, probably having no connection with the station's demise. The through lines are rusty and unused. *Bury Central Library.*

Ex-LYR 'pug' 51218 at Knowsley Street goods yard in the early summer of 1963, close to the Co-operative Bakery. The loco had been en route to Swansea from Horwich travelling as a dead engine with her rods removed, and as part of a freight train. A hot axle box detained the pug at Bury and it was sent back to Bolton, where a wheel-drop was available, for attention. *R. S. Greenwood.*

The subjects of this photograph are the LYR water crane and the BR(LMR) footbridge at the western end of Knowsley Street station. The date is 25th May 1970, shortly before the wholesale demolition of the place. The cameraman has chosen a gloomy setting in a generally gloomy station at the best of times, to provide us with a retrospective and atmospheric view of the location as it used to be. *Tom Wray.*

Knowsley Street station, 30th August 1970. Preserved Class 5 No. 44806 appeared at Helmshore for the East Lancashire Railway Preservation Society open day. The following day, the locomotive returned to Accrington and was finally brought back to Bury, 'still in steam', by Derby Type 2 D5198 (later Class 25 No. 25048). In 1970, the station infrastructure was still largely intact minus its canopies. *R. J. Farrell.*

The other side of the bridge which carried Knowsley Street over the railway: this is the west face on 25th May 1970. The four lines through the station read from left to right as, Up Slow, Up Through, Down Through and Down Slow. The lines curving to the left carried traffic on to the East Fork and thence to Bolton Street station. Note missing signal arm - a portent of the demise of the route to Bolton. The through lines are out of use. *Tom Wray.*

By the Spring of 1971, the station was all but demolished. In this view, only the covered footbridge and the Up and Down platform steps remain as everything around them are reduced to rubble. Knowsley Street had never been a handsome station, but despite its ordinary, sombre appearance, the 'low-level' amenity had character. *Bury Central Library.*

WEEKDAY TRAFFIC MOVEMENTS at KNOWSLEY STREET 1951 continued-

Train		Arr.	Dep.	Destination
21.35	Hollinwood	00.20	00.50	Aintree
21.25	Wyre Dock	01.37	01.37	Moston
00.20	Kearsley	01.22	01.50	Healey Mills
23.18	Blackburn	01.55	02.10	Moston
22.15	Goole	02.13	02.13	Aintree
01.45	Brewery	02.33	02.50	Bacup
00.25	Wigan	02.52	——	KNOWSLEY STREET
00.25	Accrington	02.12	02.55	Moston
00.44	Mytholmroyd	03.55	——	KNOWSLEY STREET
00.34	Halifax	03.06	03.30	Bolton
01.35	Aintree	03.55	04.22	Dean Lane
01.40	Crofton	04.27	04.29	Garston
04.25	Bullfield	04.49	04.49	Healey Mills
05.07	Rochdale	05.22	05.23	Bolton (Trinity St)
05.15	Bolton (Trinity St)	05.32	05.33	Rochdale
06.00	Bury (Bolton St)	06.02	06.03	Rochdale
05.55	Rochdale	06.13	06.14	Bury (Bolton St)
04.40	Brewery	05.44	06.18	Bradley Fold
03.20	Crofton	06.28	06.28	Fazakerley
06.18	Bolton (Trinity St)	06.32	06.33	Rochdale
03.20	Carlton	06.38	06.38	Aintree
00.50	Preston	05.10	06.38	Werneth
04.44	Mytholmroyd	06.03	06.45	Ramsbottom
04.25	Horbury Junction	06.48	06.54	Garston
06.40	Bolton (Trinity St)	06.58	06.59	Rochdale
06.26	Manchester (Vic)	07.01	07.04	Ramsbottom
06.00	Westhoughton	07.07	07.09	Healey Mills
07.00	Rochdale	07.16	07.17	Bolton (Trinity St)
07.05	Ramsbottom	07.18	07.20	Manchester (Vic)
07.09	Bolton (Trinity St)	07.24	07.25	Rochdale
06.58	Bacup	07.35	07.36	Manchester (Vic)
07.40	Bolton (Trinity St)	07.53	07.54	Rochdale
05.35	Bolton (Rose Hill)	07.14	07.57	Tottington Junc (Bury)
07.37	Manchester (Vic)	08.11	08.13	Bacup
07.37	Bacup	08.12	08.14	Manchester (Vic)
08.04	Rochdale	08.22	08.23	Bolton (Trinity St)
08.15	Bolton (Trinity St)	08.29	08.30	Rochdale
00.35	Goole	07.50	08.30	Bolton
07.25	Brewery	08.07	08.31	Burnley
08.42	KNOWSLEY STREET	——	08.42	Heap Bridge
08.50	KNOWSLEY STREET	——	08.50	Outwood Sidings
08.47	Bolton (Trinity St)	08.59	09.00	Rochdale
08.47	Rochdale	09.03	09.04	Bolton (Trinity St)
08.23	Bacup	09.03	——	KNOWSLEY STREET
08.38	Manchester (Vic)	09.10	——	KNOWSLEY STREET
09.06	Bolton (Trinity St)	09.17	09.18	Rochdale
09.00	Bacup	09.36	——	KNOWSLEY STREET
07.45	Aintree	09.44	09.44	Normanton
09.41	Bolton (Trinity St)	09.50	09.51	Rochdale
09.56	Bolton (Trinity St)	10.05	10.06	Rochdale
10.00	Rochdale	10.17	10.18	Bolton (Trinity St)
10.20	KNOWSLEY STREET	——	10.20	Bacup (Goods)
10.22	KNOWSLEY STREET	——	10.22	Bury Gas Works
10.00	Bolton (Halliwell)	10.31	10.31	Sharleston
09.57	Bacup	10.33	——	KNOWSLEY STREET
08.50	Horwich	10.25	10.53	Moston
10.55	Bury Gas Works	11.02	——	KNOWSLEY STREET
11.02	Tottington Junction	11.10	11.10	Crofton Hall
11.00	Rochdale	11.14	11.15	Bolton (Trinity St)
10.15	Euxton	11.38	11.40	Pontefract
11.05	Bacup	11.43	——	KNOWSLEY STREET
11.40	Rochdale	11.56	11.57	Bolton (Trinity St)
11.45	Bolton (Trinity St)	11.57	11.58	Rochdale
12.05	KNOWSLEY STREET	——	12.05	Bacup
11.00	Mytholmroyd	12.40	12.40	Fazakerley
12.37	Bolton (Trinity St)	12.51	12.52	Rochdale
12.15	Bacup	12.55	13.02	Manchester (Vic)
12.37	Bolton (Halliwell)	13.08	13.08	Healey Mills
09.15	Carlton	13.10	13.15	Garston
13.25	Rochdale	13.40	13.41	Bolton (Trinity St)
13.00	Rose Hill Junction	13.19	13.42	Littleborough
10.20	Mytholmroyd	13.20	14.00	Ramsbottom
13.55	Bolton (Trinity St)	14.09	14.10	Rochdale
11.15	Crofton	14.24	14.24	Edge Hill
14.03	Bacup	14.40	14.43	Manchester (Vic)
14.32	Rochdale	14.47	14.48	Bolton (Trinity St)
12.20	Mirfield (T,ThO)	15.04	15.10	Widnes
13.30	Aintree	15.30	15.30	Neville Hill

Train		Arr.	Dep.	Destination
12.39	Edge Hill (MWF)	15.59	15.59	Healey Mills
15.50	Rochdale	16.06	16.07	Bolton (Trinity St)
16.10	Heap Bridge	16.22	——	KNOWSLEY STREET
16.25	Rochdale	16.39	16.40	Bolton (Trinity St)
16.32	Bolton (Trinity St)	16.48	16.49	Rochdale
16.35	Rochdale	16.50	16.51	Bolton (Trinity St)
16.48	Bolton (Trinity St)	16.58	16.59	Rochdale
16.40	Bacup	17.18	17.19	Manchester (Vic)
17.13	Bolton (Trinity St)	17.29	17.30	Rochdale
17.15	Rochdale	17.31	17.32	Bolton (Trinity St)
15.32	Mytholmroyd	17.06	17.37	Bolton (Bullfield)
17.17	Manchester (Vic)	17.48	——	KNOWSLEY STREET
17.40	Bolton (Trinity St)	17.54	17.55	Rochdale
17.42	Rochdale	17.59	18.00	Bolton (Trinity St)
17.33	Bacup	18.13	18.18	Manchester (Vic)
18.00	Rochdale	18.19	18.20	Bolton (Trinity St)
14.12	Colne	18.20	18.20	Moston
18.15	Bolton (Trinity St)	18.27	18.28	Rochdale
16.50	Bacup	18.25	18.35	Moston
18.22	Radcliffe (Central)	18.43	——	KNOWSLEY STREET
18.12	Manchester (Vic)	18.45	18.47	Bacup
18.37	Rochdale	18.55	18.56	Bolton (Trinity St)
18.12	Bacup	18.52	19.00	Manchester (Vic)
18.10	Castleton (East Jct)	19.02	——	KNOWSLEY STREET
19.03	Bolton (Trinity St)	19.17	19.18	Rochdale
18.20	Rochdale (Goods)	19.10	19.25	Hellifield
19.05	Manchester (Vic)	19.37	19.39	Bacup
19.25	Rochdale	19.44	19.45	Bolton (Trinity St)
18.45	Helmshore (ThO)	19.16	19.45	Moston (livestock)
19.58	Bury (Bolton St Gds)	20.04	——	KNOWSLEY STREET
20.08	Bolton (Trinity St)	20.21	20.22	Rochdale
20.05	Rochdale	20.22	——	KNOWSLEY STREET
19.50	Bacup	20.30	20.40	Manchester (Vic)
19.20	Woodlands Road	20.36	——	KNOWSLEY STREET
20.35	Rochdale	20.50	20.51	Bolton (Trinity St)
20.35	Ramsbottom	20.54	20.54	Wentworth
20.25	Manchester (Vic)	20.58	21.05	Bacup
20.56	Bolton (Trinity St)	21.12	21.13	Rochdale
19.30	Aintree	21.27	21.27	Crofton Hall
21.25	Rochdale	21.46	21.52	Bolton (Trinity St)
21.15	Bacup	21.52	21.54	Manchester (Vic)
21.45	Bolton (Trinity St)	21.58	21.59	Rochdale
21.23	Manchester (Vic)	21.55	22.00	Bacup
20.05	Brewery	21.08	22.08	Tottington Junction
18.40	Bacup	21.32	22.12	Oldham Road
19.15	Crofton	22.38	22.38	Fazakerley
22.17	Manchester (Vic)	22.49	22.51	Bury (Bolton St)
22.42	Bolton (Trinity St)	22.54	22.55	Rochdale
22.55	Rochdale	23.12	——	KNOWSLEY STREET
22.00	Rochdale (Goods)	22.27	23.18	Blackburn
21.55	Rose Hill Junction	22.13	23.20	Healey Mills
23.20	KNOWSLEY STREET	——	23.20	Rochdale (Goods)
20.02	Brighouse	23.34	00.01	Aintree
22.45	Aintree	23.57	23.57	Healey Mills

Key:- **Arr** - Arrival time; **Dep** - Departure time; **MWF** - Monday, Wednesday, Friday; **ThO** - Thursday Only; **TThO** - Tuesday & Thursday Only.
Train timings underlined are freight. Where freight arrival and departure timings are the same this indicates train passing through without stopping.
24 Hour clock used throughout.

0-6-0T No.47584 crosses the bridge spanning the Knowsley St. - Bolton line and heads towards Bolton St. station on a cold winter's day in 1962. *R.J.Farrell.*

BUCKLEY WELLS - SUMMER AND WINTER

(opposite top) **Buckley Wells Coal Sidings as seen from Belle Vue Terrace footbridge, 6th July 1963.** 2-6-0 No.42901 approaches Bury Bolton Street station, with a train of non-corridor excursion stock for an unknown destination, reporting number 1T74. Notice the overgrown nature of the Buckley Wells Coal Sidings which have by now fallen into disuse, and the rear end of the engine shed, showing the offices, workshops and mess rooms. *R. J. Farrell.*

(right) Angle Sidings, 2nd February 1963. Although it is a quiet moment on the main line, two Metro-Camm d.m.u's pause between duties in the sidings. Projecting skywards from right to left are the public baths chimney; the Parish Church spire and Peel Mill chimney; the roof of the old ELR headquarters can be made out behind the bridge above the signalbox. The bridge parapet at the foot of the photograph marks the Bolton to Rochdale line which passed under (left to right) at this point. *R. J. Farrell.*

(opposite bottom) 'Crab' 42700 draws away from Bolton Street past Bury South signal box and over the Bolton - Rochdale line, with a Holiday week train in 1963. *R. J. Farrell.*

(right) Angle Sidings. A four-car e.m.u. of the BR Wolverton stock takes the fast line out of Bolton Street station, bound for Manchester Victoria. The electric train has just crossed the Down line from platform 4. To the right is a Cravens 2-car d.m.u., temporarily stabled on the "Coal Siding". The bridge over the Bolton - Rochdale line can be clearly seen to have had stone abutments and pilasters, the parapet and span being of metal construction. The double-gabled building to the left of the Baptist Church are numbers 22 - 28 Tenterden Street, probably offices in the 1960's. *R. J. Farrell.*

(opposite top) The Down slow line out of Bolton Street station closed in September 1965 and was relegated to a short stub with access from platform 4. The bridge over the Bolton line was then rebuilt for to carry two lines only, the Up and Down fast. In this photograph we see new railed parapet which has replaced the original portion of deck where the Down slow line would have crossed the bridge. Work is now taking place on the Up side. *R. J. Farrell.*

(right) An excellent view of Bury South signal box (formely Bury Bolton Street South) and immediate surroundings in 1978. The cabin's location is described as being in the angle between the main Up line and Bury East Fork curve 68 yards south of a previous box of 1872. As LYR 311, it was opened in 1910, measuring 30ft x 12ft x 8ft on a brick base with its rear facing Angle Sidings. Originally the L&Y built frame held 58 levers but during rationalisation in the 1960's these were gradually reduced in number. Notice the sleeper-sided coal bunker, well-stocked with fuel and the concrete slab utility hut, both anachronisms in 1978. The box closed in March 1980, but survives today after restoration by the ELR in 1992/3. *Bury Central Library.*

(opposite bottom) The date, as for the previous photograph, is the 9th October 1965. Workmen, without high-visibility vests, remove the ballast from the Up loop in preparation for the removal of the existing parapet. The new parapet rails are already in place and the narrowed bridge was from this date to carry two roads only. While workmen take advantage of some Sunday work, a green liveried BR class 504 2-car e.m.u. leaves Bolton Street station en route for Manchester. *R. J. Farrell.*

(below) A late 1960's view looking down line towards Bolton Street station. EE.Type 4 D232 draws out of Bolton Street on a sunny autunm morning with an unidentified eight coach train past South Box and Angle Sidings. Note the changes which have taken place to the searchlight signals: the spur occupied by the e.m.u. (the truncated Down slow) bereft of its colour lights. Evidence of the work being carried out in the previous photographs on the bridge spanning the Bolton - Rochdale line can be seen. *R. J. Farrell.*

Buckley Wells Crossing signal box and level crossing in 1978. This LMS box was opened in 1949 having been built on site behind the previous LYR 1872 box (the latter demolished in January 1949), then slid forward on rails to replace the old box in exactly the same position. It was closed on 16th March 1980 and demolished in April of the following year. The unkempt and weed-infested condition of the crossing area gives the impression of under use but in fact the actual crossing is on the opposite side of the fence to the left. The gates in view are part of a very unusual layout and are a double set required to span the three tracks of railway; however the protected roadway was only narrow and so the northernmost gate of each set closed outwards when not in use for road traffic. *Bury Central Library.*

Bury shed front and yard 1937, appearing somewhat bereft of locomotives, there being but one occupant. Note how the engine shed blended into the western wall of the e.m.u. works, and that the roof, (although never being basically altered throughout the life of the shed), possessed eight rows of turret vents. To the extreme left of the view, the original LYR Buckley Wells signal box can be seen, a similar structure to the one at Hagside, probably dating from the 1870's. The girder-like structure structure beyond the box is part of the overhead travelling crane which served Atherton's timber yard. *R.M.Casserley.*

(above) **A long-distance view of Bury shed and the western elevation of the e.m.u. shed, at sometime in the mid 1950s. The brick building with a squat square chimney housed the sand-drying plant, its front end appearing to have had repairs done to it. The shed yard is far from busy though the shed is well occupied, a G3 0-8-0 and an exL&Y 0-6-0 occupy the right hand road.** *B. Roberts per J. A. Peden coll.*

(right) **In contrast, to the 1937 scene, the shed here has at least six occupants, one of which can be identified as Stanier 3MT 2-6-2 No.40208. The period is late 1950s. Close inspection of the photograph reveals that the shed front is laced with scaffolding, suggesting the possibility of major maintenance work. The two right-hand roof tops have had the turret vents dismantled.** *LYR Society Collection.*

(right) **LYR 2-6-2 radial tank engine No.1450 between duties in the shed yard at Bury. There is no known date of this photograph, but presumably it was taken in Pre-Grouping days. This engine was one of a batch of 20 designed by Hoy to work on the stiff gradients on the Manchester - Oldham and Rochdale - Bacup lines, and to haul trains on such lines in direct competition with street trams. The big side tanks were suspectible to leakage and evidence of that fact is shown below the engine's numberplate. 1450 was the last in the batch, built in August 1904, becoming LMS No.11716 and withdrawn August 1926. To the right is the buffer beam of a 'Pug', a type not too familiar with Bury. The building to the rear is the west elevation of the central portion of the carriage shed.** *J.Hooper coll.*

This well-turned out specimen is one of Hoy's 2-6-2 radial tank engines No.1441 at Bury shed on some unknown date. Completed on 7th April 1904, the engine was withdrawn from service as LMS No. 11707 August 1926. Bury appears to have had two of these specimens during most of the life of the class. *Bury Central Library.*

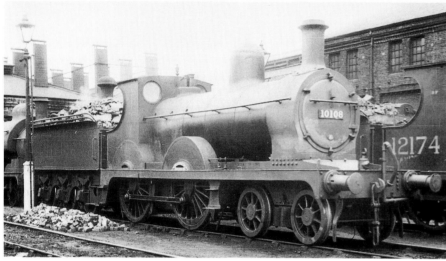

Barton Wright L&Y 4-4-0 No.10108 was allocated to Bury in the late 1920s. Built in 1888, this engine was numbered 984 before Grouping and along with the rest of the thirty strong class had all been withdrawn by 1935.

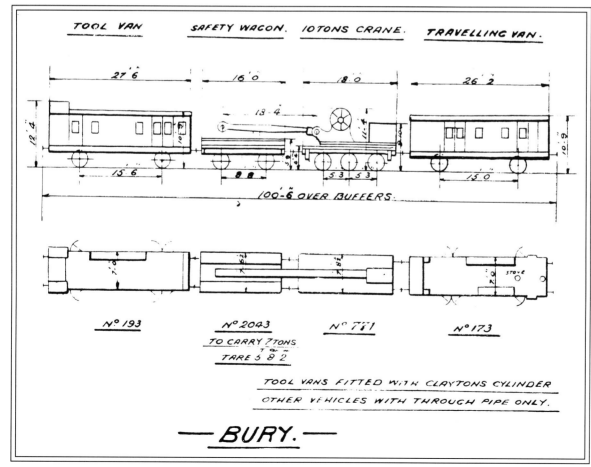

The Lancashire & Yorkshire Railway saw fit to equip Bury with a breakdown train which included a 10 tons capacity hand crane. This same train saw service into the LMS period and the vans had an extended life into BR days. No steam crane was ever allocated to Bury, Newton Heath providing their 50 tonner for any heavy lifts in the area. The train's operational range encompassed the area roughly covered by this survey.

Probably the mainstay of Bury's motive power stud from the turn of the century up to the mid 1950's were the Aspinall L&Y 0-6-0's. Over 400 of these locomotives were built between 1889 and 1917. After Grouping the LMS sent them countrywide but the majority stayed within the old 'Lanky' boundary. 12382 (previously LYR 685) seen on Bury shed yard in 1936, was allocated to the shed for most of its working life.

A close-up view of Bury shed on 24th April 1951 with two tank engines, one identified as Stanier 2-6-4T 42476. This engine seems ready for duty, its bunker full, while the sister engine takes water. Note the 'lion and wheel' BR emblem on the tank side, the LYR water columns, and the shed roof which had by this date, lost several rows of vents. This was the stuff that ex-LYR engine sheds were made of. *H.C.Casserley.*

(below) Ex-LYR electric unit, BR No. M28708, stabled on the sidings of the e.m.u. shop, 28th September 1958. Their useful life over, having run the Manchester to Bury line for thirty years, they now await disposal. The unit in the fore-ground is an unidentified First Class Control Trailer which could seat 72 in its 63ft 7in. length. *F. W. Shuttleworth, LYR Society Collection.*

A much later view of Bury shed during its function as a storage facility for electric locomotives and units, 2nd April 1972. To the left is E26000 TOMMY, shorn of its nameplates and a long way from its usual haunts on the Manchester - Sheffield line. To the locomotive's right is electric multiple unit M77163. Notice the apparently good condition of the shed roof and the white defunct water columns. *Locofotos.*

A general view of the shed and some of its 'stored' occupants in the early 1970's. The fabric of the place basucally unchanged for nearly a century. *W. T. Stubbs Collection.*

(left) A contemporary view of part of the eastern side of the electric multiple unit shop, southern end, summer 1993. The purpose of the rod projecting from the wall and extending over the siding defies explanation. The original setts of the yard which were once part of the surface on the eastern side are still in situ, the yard now traversed by an expanded metal fence. *Author's collection.*

(below) The front end of the e.m.u. shop as it is today, following its use by GEC/Alsthom during their work on Metrolink. The building is now Grade 2 listed thereby protected from demolition or modification. *Author's collection.*

Chapter 3. BURY BOLTON STREET TO RAMSBOTTOM

Whether your destination was Rawtenstall, Bacup, Accrington or Helmshore, Bury's ELR station was the place to start the journey. On departing, the train had to pass beneath the booking hall and offices which straddled the line, and then immediately entered Bolton Street Tunnel, all 80 yards of it, and emerged at the north portal, directly opposite the Castle Armoury on the right. To the right also, in a recess in the retaining wall stood Bolton Street North signal box (LYR wood 1909) and following the curve of the retaining wall, three coal sidings trailed away from the Up slow line. To the left, the much more extensive Castlecroft goods yard, the so-called "EL" yard, which owed its existence to the East Lancashire Railway. Here, seven curved sidings fanned out across the yard, each one having entered by way of a series of trailing points off the down goods loop.

The climbing gradient from the station was 1 in 377 and this continued up to the first crossing of the Irwell at Burrs. Four tracks headed north from the Castlecroft area, along an embankment which carried the railway to Tottington Junction. Beyond Castlecroft, the line crossed Tanpits Road; to the right was Peel Tannery and to the left an area of rough land (now the site of Hare Structural Steel - "California Works") and Bury Power Station, now demolished, the land it once occupied taken by Chamberhall 33kv substation. Bury Corporation Electricity Works

had two sidings which trailed back from the start of the Holcombe Brook Branch opposite Peel Mills. The sidings closest to the works ran beneath an awning for its full length and emerged at a dead-end a few yards further on. Near Chamberhall Street bridge, this siding ran over a weigh bridge whilst a cross-over connected to the second siding which ran back about two-thirds of the works. This siding was apparently used to store wagons which were employed to convey power station fly-ash. A spoil tip separated the main Down line from these two sidings.

A brick road bridge marked the crossing of Chamberhall Street (actually a 'Tunnel' beneath the railway). Tottington Junction was marked by Tottington Junction signal box, (LYR/LMS 1923) which controlled a mini complex of sidings amidst a jumble of industry: Bury Power Station, Peel Mills (1885) and Fernhill Chemical Works to the left, and a set of sidings serving Bury Saw Mills (now Raab Karcher Timber) which had its own overhead travelling crane.

The main line had now reverted to double track and curved gently north west, passing under a metal bridge which linked the chemical works with Park Road. Opposite the works, was Bury Corporation Yard which also had its own sidings accessed by a long approach line running up a steep slope. This approach line made a connection with

One of the first features to attract attention on leaving Bolton Street station for the journey north to Ramsbottom was Peel Mill. The construction of Peel No.1 Mill was probably the main focus of interest for the cameraman during its final stages of construction circa 1886/1887. The mill belonged to Peel Spinning & Manufacturing Co. Ltd. and is said to have "inaugurated a new era in the history of Bury". Its six storeys were reduced to three in 1963. The railway between Bury and Ramsbottom predated the mill by forty years. On the right in the photograph, adjacent to the Up main line, stood Bury (EL) No.3 signal box, having been erected in 1882 (as LYR 309) and originally named Bury Junction 'A'. It was renamed Bury EL No.3 in between 1891 and 1902, and closed in 1923. Beyond the line of wagons a second signal box stands on the newly opened Tottington Branch (1882). This was Bury (EL) No.4 signal box (LYR 360) and had the merit of being renamed twice to Tottington Junction 'B' (1891-1902) and Tottington Branch Sidings (1909). As Bury EL No.4, it had opened in 1882 and was closed in 1925. The large allotment, with its substantial buildings, was permanent enough to be shown on Ordnance Survey plans dated 1893. *Bury Central Library.*

A sylvan scene at Summerseat, 5th September 1966. This view, looking towards Bury, belies the fact that within a relatively short distance south from here, the scene changes completely to the far from sylvan urban area of Bury. The footbridge was a short-lived addition to the station, removed sometime after 1970. *P.E.Baughan, M.Blakemore coll.*

the main line near Fernhill siding signal box (1901). Quite near, to the left; the ever-present Irwell flowed parallel, the railway looking down on it from the safety of the embankment. Open land could now be seen on both sides: to the left, the flood plain of the river, to the right, a steep-sided bluff overlooking the railway. A cluster of houses and Joseph Barden's glue works (Calrow's Mill) appear at Higher Woodhill to the left. Here, the line crossed the river twice on ex-LYR bridges: the first bridge was the longer, consisting a metal girder with twin stone skewed arches at either end; the second bridge consisting of a metal girder with a single stone arch at either end. This bridge also crossed the old road between Limefield and Burrs, the road actually passing through the northern arch.

The village of Burrs could be seen whilst travelling between these two bridges on an embankment overlooking water meadows; Burrs: a cluster of houses; the Brown Cow public house, and Peel & Yates Bleach Works.

Beyond Burrs, the railway curved gently to the north west, the Irwell now seen to form one of its large meanders, enclosing meadow land and the up-standing Castle Steads, the site of a Roman Fort. From here, the line passed through Touchy Hill Cutting, a fifty feet deep man-made gash in the hillside, spanned by a wooden footbridge which was supported on brick piers. Out of the cutting, the river appeared once again on the left, with Springside Farm to the right. Here, a stream issued from Balldinstone Reservoir and trickled into the parent river. The railway was now carried on an embankment separating quarry excavations and reservoirs from the river near Wood Road hamlet - a

group of cottages and a cotton mill. Olive Siding signal box (1874) once marked the position of Olive's Siding, which amounted to nothing more than a looped siding of the down line. At the end of Olive's Siding, the main line entered Summerseat Cutting; this is the location of Chest Wheel Bridge over the Irwell, from which a footpath passed beneath the line from Hall O'th'Hill to Bury Road.

On leaving Summerseat Cutting, a small goods yard appeared on the right, complete with stone goods shed with a through siding and two short, curved lines serving as a coal siding. At Twist Bridge, the Irwell swung away from the railway at 90 degrees, the latter crossing Railway Street bridge before entering Summerseat Station, (opened by the ELR on 25th June 1846).

The station consisted of two slightly curved platforms, the Up side possessing the station buildings (booking office, porter's room and gents), which faced the junction of Miller Street and Rowlands Road. The Down platform made do with a wooden shelter and awning, and at the far end of this platform ramp stood Summerseat Station signal box (LYR wood 1922). Harrison and Sale's Guide referred to the ELR station as a "roadside halt", consisting of no more than a wooden hut perched on the ground. The LYR improved the amenity as public patronage increased. Certainly by 1890, the platforms were raised to normal height, although on the rail side of the station building, the original low-level platform remained.

The line continued to curve northwards, carried on a lengthy embankment which sloped on the west side down to an area covered by Ramsbottom UDC sewage works. To the right, Miller Street ran along-

(right) **The 3.30 p.m. Bacup - Bury service emerges into daylight briefly between Nuttall tunnel and Brooksbottom tunnel, 9th April 1963. The walled lane on the left is Starling Street leading up to Nuttall hamlet and Nuttall Hall Farm. The stone chimney belonged to Nuttall Mill, a common feature of early mills to site their chimney on elevated ground to increase the fire draught and create greater boiler furnace heat.** *I.G.Holt.*

(below) **Ramsbottom station facing north, 23rd April 1959. It is a slack time, the gates closed to rail traffic. A porter on the Up platform, glances across to two seated gents on the Down platform. The signal box, crossing gate, footbridges and a platform weighing machine can be seen from the Down platform, on a spring day 35 years ago.** *H.C.Casserley.*

side the line to a row of terraced houses near a second and larger goods shed. The 1937 plan shows that there was a looped siding running parallel to the Down line, the goods yard and shed standing on the up side and served by three sidings and a headshunt. The dominant feature, however, was reserved for the 200 yards long Brooksbottom Viaduct (No.40), spanning the Irwell with ten stone arches of 31 feet span. Six arches were on the south side of the river, the main river span being a metal girder about 93 feet long. This girder was supported midway by a stone pier which rose from the river bed. From the Brooksbottom side, the pier can be seem to contain two through arches akin to the shape of a church window. Like other viaducts described in this book, Brooksbottom Viaduct is still there to be marvelled at today and fortunately serving a useful function in carrying the Bury to Rawtenstall ELR line.

Another striking feature was the riverside Brooksbottom Mill (1773), also known as Hoyle's Mill since the business within its walls was owned by Joshua Hoyle and Sons from 1872. Before leaving 'Brox', (the local name for Brooksbottom), the line passed rows of terraced houses arranged regularly on Garden Street, Thorn Street, India Street and others, all Hoyle's houses and originally back-to-back. These could be seen to the left just before the line plunged into Brooksbottom Tunnel (423 yards), a curved bore through Rossendale rock which formed a shoulder of land on the west side of the Irwell Valley.

At the village of Nuttall, daylight was restored briefly, as the line passed through a short but steep-sided cutting before entering Nuttall Tunnel, a curved neighbour of Brooksbottom Tunnel, 115 yards long and noted for its corbel-decorated north end portal. From here, the line continued in a deep cutting which receded, allowing a view of Ocean Chemical Works, formerly John Grant's printing works.

Before crossing the Irwell for the penultimate time prior to reaching Ramsbottom, the line crossed first Nuttall Old Goit which supplied water to a chemical works: this crossing point was marked either side of the railway by stone parapets of unusual shape. Then the river was spanned by a 102 feet girder bridge which had stone abutments and two central stone piers. On the right was Nuttall Park with its tennis courts, bowling greens and bandstand. Here, the line kept to a shal-

low embankment before crossing the Irwell again on Square River Bridge, another ex-LYR girder bridge of 54 feet span, supported at each end by stone abutments. Here too was a subway of 7 feet span and very low headroom, straight-sided and arched. It is still there and used by strollers between Ramsbottom and Nuttall Park.

To the left was Holme Mill (1912), now occupied by Cormar Carpets, and then Square Works, roughly 241 feet square, but not exactly a perfect quadrilateral! This was owned by Messrs Hepburn since 1867 for the purpose of bleaching cotton. The final approach into Ramsbottom was no less full of interest. To the end, the line crossed water on a low viaduct which carried the railway over Square Works reservoirs - the viaduct known as Square Reservoir Bridge. Close to the head of the reservoir stood Ramsbottom South signal box (LYR wood 1904) which replaced the earlier Ramsbottom Warehouse box of 1891 and was itself replaced by two ground frames after 1938.

The cricket ground to the right, with pavilion and bandstand, marked the leisure amenities for Ramsbottom people; to the left, down-to-earth, if not satanic, the monoliths of long hours of graft, Cobden Mill, Meadow Mill, Crow Mill and Railway Mill. You had arrived in Ramsbottom.

Ex-LYR (No.685) 0-6-0 3F LMS No.12382 pauses with crew to have an official photograph taken on 8th February 1937. Official records describe the event as train "consisting of 25 wagons loaded with cylinders for use in paper mills". The exact location is not given; a brief reference to "Bury Goods" is made which is both vague and unhelpful. However, it is thought that the chimney bearing the triple letter 'H' 1905, belonged to Harvey's Peel Tannery, thus fixing the scene near the bridge over Tanpits Road in Bury. Therefore we begin our illustrative journey to Ramsbottom. *NRM (DY 21964).*

A contemporary view of bridge No.34 which carries the Bury to Ramsbottom line over the Irwell at Burrs. The view is towards Bury.

Another present day view of the metal span bridge, No.35, over the Irwell at Burrs. The arch, bridge No.36, allows Hows Lane to pass under the railway.

Summerseat station, 23rd April 1954. The view is towards Bury. Features of interest when the station was in full-swing included the low-level ELR platform which existed at the southern end of the station, the whitewashed borders around the 'gardens', and the mineral wagons standing alongside the original ELR goods shed. The small glazed structure with a double pitched roof was possibly a small waiting room and not a signal box as is often stated. *H.C.Casserley.*

(right) Summerseat 4th August 1953. Aspinall 2P 50647, still going strong propelling a push-pull service from Bacup to Bury. The ex-LYR engine, was withdrawn in February 1959 after sixty years service. Here, a siding connection trailed back from the Down line by the barrow crossing. *F.W.Shuttleworth, LYR Soc. coll.*

(below) Summerseat station, looking north from the footbridge, 5th September 1966. The signalman in the box appears to have been very quick to lower his signal as the Cravens 2-car d.m.u. enters the station. The signal box opened in September 1922 replacing an 1875 box which stood on the Up side platform north of the station buildings. *P.E.Baughan, M.Blakemore coll.*

Summerseat station from the low-level Up platform, looking north in 1965. When manned, this must have been one of the most pleasant places to work, especially during the summer months when this photograph captured the scene. The lattice footbridge was erected in the early 1960's. *Ramsbottom Heritage Centre.*

The scene at Summerseat one day in January 1967. An angry crowd demonstrate against the reduction in services on the Rawtenstall to Bury line. Several arrests were made. News of the service reduction had been made public in December 1966. "The Revised Rail Service Commencing Monday 5th December 1966", left Summerseat with 12 Down and 13 Up trains, Monday to Friday, with no Sunday service. *M.Blakemore coll.*

The southern portal of Nuttall tunnel, post-1973 when the route to Rawtenstall from Bury was singled and was used by coal trains running from the Yorkshire coalfield to the Rawtenstall Coal Concentration plant. *D.Ibbotson, LYR Soc. coll.*

A contemporary (1992) view of Brooksbottom viaduct which spanned the valley of the Irwell. This view shows the eastern aspect at the southern end. Although dressed stone was used almost exclusively, the arched rings are of brick. The central metal span is hidden by vegetation, although two of the northern most arches to Brooksbottom tunnel can be discerned. *Author's coll.*

(below) A somewhat atmospheric scene on the approach to Ramsbottom in 1955. The three-coach train is destined for Colne, taking the line via Accrington and Burnley, hauled by BR Standard 4MT 75049 on a Sunday morning service. *B.Roberts, J.A.Peden coll.*

Chapter 4. RAMSBOTTOM

"Station and the manufacturing village of that name, four miles from Bury, beautifully situated in the picturesque Valley of Ramsbottom; and here the fine view of the country is seen flanked by Holcombe Hill, on the one hand, and by beautifully wooded rising ground, on the other, on the summit of which stands the Grants' Tower"
Harrison & Sale's Guide 1846.

Ramsbottom was important enough to merit its own historical description. Between 1851 and 1881, the population of the town increased by 89%, from 2,224 souls to 4,205, a recognisably rapid increase. In 1848, Ramsbottom possessed five mills dealing with either cotton or wool and by 1884, the total number of mills had risen to fourteen. Several new industries had entered the town including paper and chemicals manufacture. The Town was a veritable 19th century growth-point and probably owes the fact to the entrepreneurial spirit of its local people and as much to the arrival of the railway.

In terms of industry, one works alone provides a good example of the base upon which Ramsbottom flourished. Square Works, which stood close to the railway on the south side of the town, owed its existence to the Grant Brothers who opened the "Square Calico Printing Works" in 1821. Such was their dependence on the nearby railway that a siding agreement had been established in 1857. And such was the influence of the Grant family in the town generally that money collected from a toll gate on Bridge Street, a short distance east of the crossing, was reputedly used to maintain Peel Brow Bridge (now Ramsbottom Bridge).

Ramsbottom station opened on the 28th September 1846 and was positioned adjacent to the level crossing on the south side of Bridge Street. Its importance was assured when the Extension Line to Accrington and the Bacup Branch necessitated a change of train to be made here because the platforms of Stubbins station only served the lines of the Bacup branch. On either side of the station were sidings. On the down side was a stone goods shed which adjoined the platform plus a signal box built on to the goods shed wall, known appropriately as "Warehouse Cabin". On the up side were sidings which served Ramsbottom Paper Mill and a very early East Lancashire Railway one-road engine shed, very little of which is known about. The goods sidings were found to be inadequate by the 1880s.

"Local Board Minutes of the 1880s make frequent reference to the insufficient goods accommodation near Ramsbottom Station. This was later remedied by the extension of the goods yard between Ramsbottom and Stubbins". *Stephanie Hamilton M.A. Thesis 1974.*

As early as 1846, the town made national news by dint of a report in the *Manchester Guardian* (May 20th) relating an episode of rioting between rival gangs of navvies who were at work on the line.

"An alarming riot took place among the labourers on the East Lancashire Railway at Ramsbottom. Disturbances arose from a dispute respecting wages between two English and two Irish labourers (in the Grant Arms) who, as previous jealously had existed between the two nations, succeeded in enlisting their respective countrymen into the quarrels and nearly 2000 men were at one time engaged".

A copy of an LYR plan of 1913 showing Ramsbottom station area reveals the infrastructure centred on and adjacent to the station. The main station building, containing the larger number of facilities, stood against the Up platform, with a smaller group of buildings opposite serving the Down side. Glazed canopies of ridge and furrow design overspanned the main waiting areas on both platforms supported by cast iron pillars and roof girders. The Down platform was slightly longer and backed on to the windowless stone goods shed. A sturdy LYR wooden footbridge (1893) half-glazed and roofed connected the platforms at the level crossing end of the station. P.T.L. Rees described both sides of the station as they appeared in a 1969 survey:-

"The downside structures are LYR Style 2* in design, showing all its features. The booking hall is large and cavernous with a skylight above, and the blank wall which supports the awning runs for a considerable length down the platform showing that passengers were once numerous. The up side had the original buildings comprising a station master's house and the booking offices. The construction of more offices between 1860 and 1880 altered the original layout of the buildings. During the 1890s, a third phase of building brought the LYR Style 2 across to the up side in the form of further offices with a wooden frontage". *Industrial Archaeology Vol 6 No 3.*

* Style 2 was widespread on the LYR system. Small stone or brick were used in construction, many irregular and small offices, frosted glass in square plain windows, highly ornate ironwork, and blank walls. Wood was a common material, and awnings had a toothed effect. The style is common along the line described, dating to the general refurbishment of stations carried out between 1890 and 1900.

A general view of Ramsbottom station looking north, 5th July 1964. Still gas lit and largely intact, the building was of large proportions in relation to the size of the town it served, since it was regarded as the most important station between Bury and Rawtenstall. Careful study will reveal that on the Up platform, the glazed frontage added by the LYR which blocked off the original recessed waiting area a la Perring. The Down side canopy was supported by row of cast iron columns which gently curved with the alignment of the platform. Note the lightweight welded steel footbridge which replaced the LYR timber structure. *E.Blakey, LYR Soc.*

Ramsbottom station looking south, from the pedestrian footbridge. 50829 is about to leave the station with the 6.37 p.m. to Bacup, 24th April 1955. The full extent of the LYR footbridge can be appreciated, plus the sleepered roadway forming the level crossing and the mesh-covered crossing gate on the town-side of the railway. The siding signal, track-circulated like its main line neighbour, is positioned on the footbridge roof for easier sighting by drivers. The bill-board by the side of the telephone booth advertises a 2/- return cheap rate on Saturdays to Blackburn. *B.Roberts, J.A.Peden coll.*

Between the Down platform and Railway Street was a narrow yard, complete with two yard cranes of 10 tons and 30 cwt capacity. Behind the Up platform, a setted yard extended towards the paper mill goyt, over which three dead-end sidings of different lengths passed. This yard had its opening near the main station buildings on Bridge Street guarded by a 12 ft gate. A 5 ton crane, weigh bridge and office completed the goods facilities. Ramsbottom Paper Mill (Hepburn and Co) had two sidings in the yard separated from the other three sidings by a wall. The same plan shows a wagon turntable and siding running off at right-angles and into the mill yard.

On the north side of the level crossing stood Ramsbottom Station signal box (LMS brick 1938) which replaced an LYR box of 1875. The 1938 box was built on the same site as its predecessor in a somewhat cramped area between the down line, the level crossing and the pedestrian footbridge. Beyond the box was the open lattice footbridge which enabled pedestrians to cross the railway at will even when the gates were closed to road traffic on Bridge Street.

In 1913, Ramsbottom UDC introduced a trolley bus service which served the station. The route authorised included Holcombe Brook to Edenfield and included a spur from the Market Place via Bridge Street to the station. The first public service began at 6 p.m. on August 14th 1913 with the first journey running from Ramsbottom station to Holcombe Brook. A full service then commenced a week later. However, the use of the spur was short-lived being abandoned on October 5th 1914 soon after the outbreak of the 1914-18 war. Older readers will perhaps remember the overhead which was left in place until 1924, and the "Ramsbottom UDC" crest which adorned the bus side panels

in later years. This whole service came to an end on 31st March 1931. Ramsbottom has twice been the scene of railway accidents. One of these occurred on August 18th 1923 when a sixty wagon train, running between Earby and Salford, ran out of control after passing through Helmshore and came to an abrupt stop at a siding bufferstop at which over a dozen wagons were totally smashed.

"Two of them buckled and were thrown on to the main line, but it was found possible to remove these without much delay. Three huge baulks of pitch-pine were apparently driven through the line-side cabin into a goyt, which is spanned by a footbridge within the goods yard, and but for this they might have been forced into the police station, which stands just outside the railway station". *Rossendale Free Press 18th August 1923.*

Such an incident created an evening's entertainment for those attracted to scenes of disaster.

"The pile of wreckage is one of the sights of Ramsbottom at the moment, and crowds of people are watching the operations". *RFP. Aug.18 1923.*

Yet again on Friday February 10th 1959, a runaway goods train from Rose Grove, Burnley, headed by 2-6-4T 42480, gathered speed on the Baxenden Bank and failed to stop at Ramsbottom, where it would have continued on shunting duty, and coasted on without an engine crew, they having abandoned the locomotive, and came to a stop somewhere between Summerseat and Tottington. The disgraced engine (a substitute for the usual Class 5 4-6-0) ran light engine back to Accrington probably in need of attention to the flats on its driving wheels.

Before the First World War, Square Works had substantial sidings which connected to the Down line beyond Square Reservoir bridge which carried the railway over Square Works reservoir. Shunting was carried out by the works' own engine which was housed in a shed at the end of a short spur on the west side of the building. During the Great Conflict the engine was commissioned for military purposes and returned after 1918 somewhat jaded by its wartime use. The little four-coupled saddle tank ARCHIBALD was named after Archibald Hepburn one of the owners of the bleaching company. After 1924, ARCHIBALD was replaced by an armour-plated petrol-driven locomotive (war surplus).

Ramsbottom Sorting Sidings comprised 56 roads in total, and covered a large expanse of land sandwiched between the Irwell and several industrial buildings alongside Stubbins Lane. One of these housed the trolley buses up to 1930 before assuming the role of omnibus depot. The sidings nearest Stubbins Lane were coal sidings, and consisted of four dead-end roads running south. The Sorting Sidings lay between the main running lines and the river: 16 dead-end roads ran northwards. One signal box and a ground frame controlled traffic in the sidings: Ramsbottom Up Sidings North and Ramsbottom Down Sidings GF, the latter situated at the exit from the down sidings.

Beyond the sidings the railway ran on an embankment between the Irwell and a wide goyt, crossing the latter near Ramsbottom/Stubbins Gas Works which was located on the eastern side of the railway, and having its own siding.

At the gas works, on the Up side, was Stubbins Jct. signal box (LYR brick 1900) whilst a short distance further on, the railway crossed the Bolton to Edenfield road on an oblique stone bridge before entering Stubbins Station. This bridge now shows evidence of alterations which were made in order to accommodate the Accrington line. A large double iron bracket is attached to the west side of the bridge and once supported the track bed at an angle to the original parapet. The underside of the bridge is of skewed brick, set between large stone blocks. Stubbins station marked the parting of the main line to Accrington and the branch line to Rawtenstall and Bacup.

The Down platform, Ramsbottom, looking south as Fairburn Class 4MT 2-6-4T 42153 enters the station with a train for Bacup, 23rd April 1954. This scene shows the northern end wall of the goods shed with its single arched opening through which a single siding passed towards the rear of the station. A wooden 'jimmy' or yard crane can be seen in the small goods yard, one of two which operated there. A portion of Square Mill chimney rises skyward in the background. *H.C.Casserley.*

(above) **Ramsbottom station goods shed, southern aspect, 5th July 1964. The old ELR shed is out of use; note the closed door and the rampant vegetation colonising the yard. The windowless building permitted light through the open doors and the circular ventilation holes in the end walls. The wooden sign to the right of the door reads, "No engine allowed to enter this warehouse". *E.Blakey, LYR Soc. coll.***

(below) **Ramsbottom station frontage as seen from Bridge Street. In keeping with the area it served, the building was constructed from dressed stone, probably derived from local quarries. The glazed gabled roof stood over the booking hall, the entrance to which had a small timber awning. The station footbridge is now one of the open lattice types and replaced the timber structure in 1959/60. *E.Blakey, LYR Soc. coll.***

Interior of Ramsbottom Station signal box, 6.00 p.m., 22nd August 1956. The photographer has attempted to capture the track layout board and the block instruments at the expense of maintaining a level view. At this moment in time, a down train is passing the box, the signalman giving the "train entering section" to Stubbins Jct. box. Note the track circuit instrument (second from left) reads "line occupied". There is no train on the Up line. The view is northwards, the front of the box facing the running lines, the signalman standing with his back to them. *B.Roberts, J.A.Peden coll.*

An evocative photograph of 50829 departing Ramsbottom , 26th September 1953, with a two-coach push-pull train for Bacup. The dominant feature of the scene, however, is the hefty timber, half-glazed and roofed footbridge which connected both platforms. This was removed circa 1959/60 and duly replaced with a lattice open bridge. *F.W.Shuttleworth, LYR Soc. coll.*

The 6.24 p.m. Colne - Manchester Victoria approaches Ramsbottom station on 22nd August 1956, drawn by 'Crab' 42724, an Agecroft engine. The photograph was taken from the pedestrian footbridge which stood to the north of the signal box. *B.Roberts, J.A.Peden coll.*

A posed photograph in Ramsbottom goods yard, taken behind the stone wall which lined the rear of the Down platform, circa 1920. The Edenfield firm of J & J Whittaker had served the railways for over a century when their contract for the delivery of goods to and from local stations was terminated in October 1953. The firm started carting for the LYR as soon as the Bacup Branch was opened, and dealt with traffic from all stations between Ramsbottom and Bacup. In later years, horse-power was superseded by motor lorries, at least one vehicle being kept at Ramsbottom. *Ramsbottom Heritage Centre.*

A view of the Up yard at Ramsbottom, 10th May 1955. 51504 shunts a rake of mixed wagons, overlooked by Ramsbottom Paper Mill chimney. Notice the stone-faced Up platform which at this point tapered to a narrow width at the southern end. *B.Roberts, J.A.Peden coll.*

(above) **Fowler 7F 49666 approaches Ramsbottom station on the 4.45 p.m. Bacup-Moston Sidings goods 20th
May 1955. The extensive Ramsbottom North sidings
lay beyond the long rake of vans behind the loco which
is just about to cross a bridge over a disused mill goyt.
The author remembers well 49666 trundling long
rakes of wagons such as seen here along the down gradient from Middleton Jct to Moston Sidings on frequent occasions. The locomotive always emitted a
whistling noise from the motions as she travelled on
the last leg of her journey. Others clanked; 49666
whistled. *B.Roberts, J.A.Peden coll.***

(right) **BR Standard 2-6-4T 80086 runs bunker first
across the timber level crossing in Ramsbottom circa
1955. The open lattice public footbridge and the 1938
signal box are well-illustrated in this photograph, the
more popular view often being taken from the footbridge towards the station. *Ramsbottom Heritage Centre.***

**Aspinall rebuild of a Barton-Wright Class 2F 0-6-0T
No.51504 takes the 7.40 p.m. goods from Ramsbottom
to Bury Gas Sidings on 10th May 1955. The engine is
several hundred yards out of the station and is seen
here traversing Square River bridge over the Irwell.
*B.Roberts, J.A.Peden coll.***

Chapter 5. ONWARDS TO BACUP

"The introduction of the railway into Rossendale, by increasing facilities for transport and intercommunication, gave a marked stimulus to trade and manufactures, which it may be safely assumed, could otherwise scarcely have reached their present proportions"
Thomas Newbiggin "History of the Forest of Rossendale" 1893.

Setting the scene - The hilly nature of the environment through which the railway passed between Stubbins Junction and Bacup is not Pennine in character but uniquely Rossendale. The essential geology is comprised of strata of flagstones, mudstones, shales and coal seams, the hill tops capped by coarse sandstones, the valley bottoms blanketed with glacial clay. Natural exposures of rock are few; man-made ones abound. Slopes are smooth and rounded, a product of the end of the Ice Age when ice turned to water and the valleys were inundated. Torrents filled the valleys with lakes, and where meeting up with rising ground, spilled over into neighbouring valleys to form water-worn channels.

Into the landscape came moorland farms and valley bottom booths and folds. Villages grew into small towns by virtue of their location: Haslingden, Rawtenstall, Ramsbottom, Bacup and Whitworth to name a few. Coal seams led to shallow mining and the ubiquitous flagstone was extensively quarried for paving, door steps, lintels, roofing, floors, setts and building blocks. Flagstone not only paved Rossendale's streets but was also exported to the growing towns and cities of northern England. As slate was to North Wales, so flagstone was to Rossendale. Raw wool from the moorland farms found its way downslope to the weavers' cottages and the stone-built mills. In 1869, the Irwell valley between Ramsbottom and Bacup was a thriving area. Cotton had entered the industrial scene, and all but ousting wool, formed the basis of the textile industry, in a unique blend of spinning, weaving and bleaching. Added to this was the felt industry, in existence since the 1850s, and to come by 1874 the shoe and slipper industry of the Rossendale Valley.

Not surprisingly, a reliable means of transport was deemed vital by those at the helm of industry. Roads were one means; railways were another. As every student of geography learns, transport routes in hilly areas negotiate their way through the hills by keeping to the valleys. Thereby avoiding steep slopes and inclement weather [a negative response], and to tap the desire of the populace to travel and convey goods [a positive response].

The Rossendale Valley exhibits man's ingenious ways of overcoming the capriciousness of Nature. Through Bacup, the infant Irwell is culverted and confined to man-made channels, and then with regained freedom, twists, and winds down valley towards Rawtenstall, fed on its way by minor streams, and all the while asserting its presence.

Man has had to share the Valley with the river, "so irrevocably intertwined with the railway throughout the distance", as one writer has put it. Space is limited so that roads and streets often occupy ground on the valley sides, and buildings of all kinds jostle for any flat sites. It is not without reason that "The Glen", the narrowest section of the Valley, contains fewer buildings, space only for the Irwell, the main road and the railway, the latter forced to pass through three tunnels.

South of Rawtenstall, the Irwell enters a wider valley still flanked by hills such as Holcombe and Scout Moor. Even here the river winds its way towards Bury, swinging side to side over its flood plain: the viaducts and bridges which spanned it had to be larger and sturdier: in the 1950s, there were nine main crossings of the Irwell between Ramsbottom and Rawtenstall, and several footbridges.

The historical development of the railway between Ramsbottom and Bacup has been well-documented elsewhere [see *The Bacup Branch* - LYR Society branchline publication] and it is sufficient here to provide an alternative background as seen through the eyes of contempo-rary observers. Then we can travel the line as it was before post-war development appeared, but even then it is interesting to look back to early days to illustrate what was, and to look at the route today to reveal what is left.....

An Alternative History - On the 17th august 1848, The Blackburn, Burnley, Accrington & Colne Extension Railway opened to traffic between Stubbins Junction and Accrington. Thus the 4 mile single line from Stubbins to Rawtenstall, as planned by the Manchester, Bury & Rossendale Railway, found itself reduced to a mere branch line, usurped by the more important Extension line into North East Lancashire. At Stubbins (442 ft above sea level) the main line trains passed through the junction without stopping, leaving the small station (opened in January 1847) to serve the branch line only. Passengers for Rawtenstall and the Rossendale Valley had to change at Ramsbottom station about a mile to the south. The early station at Stubbins served a small industrial community and was described in Harrison and Sale's Guide as a "roadside station", to be rebuilt in 1856 as part of the doubling of the line to Rawtenstall.

The only intermediate station between Stubbins and Rawtenstall was at Ewood Bridge, a wayside station which had been opened by the ELR on 28th September 1846. Ewood Bridge station, taking its name from the village which stands on the Edenfield to Haslington Turnpike Road, and where the latter crossed the Irwell. Perhaps the only reason for establishing a station here was as a means of interchange between the railway and road coaches which plied between Accrington, Blackburn, Clitheroe and Whalley and the towns to the south.

Rawtenstall station had opened on the 28th September 1846 and served as a single line terminus from Stubbins Junction until the 27th March 1848. In those years the ELR planned, built and operated the line; it was to be another eleven years before the Lancashire & Yorkshire Railway Company absorbed the ELR, and took over the line completely. The plan to continue the line on to Bacup was fundamental to ELR thinking: an Act of Parliament dated 27th July 1846 had authorised the extension. In the event, the single line reached only as far as Newchurch (Warth) where a station was built to serve as the new terminus from March 28th 1848. The line actually ended beyond the station, penetrating a hill a short-distance.

The incipient tunnel was described by Harrison-Sale's Guide of 1849 as follows: "...the line here terminated a little above the Newchurch Station, by an archway tunnelled into the rock for the distance of thirty or forty yards, in the side of a steep, wild and wooded height called "The Thrutch".

Further work on the 177 chain extension ceased until September 1851. Then on 29th September 1851, tenders for the extension were received as follows: Thomas Brassey £38,800; Shaw & Briggs £38,728; Taylor of Accrington £37,500; T & J Nowell £37,188; G.Thompson & Co. £34,450; A & G Holme of Liverpool £34,400; Dickson & Mackenzie of Wellington, Salop £27,845.

The last named won the contract for the line and for the quoted price, bored three tunnels, did all the civil works and laid the track. The chronology of events during construction makes informative reading.
12th April 1852. "Some delay in the tunnel works on the Bacup Branch, the masons having struck for higher wages. The rest of the works satisfactorily 504 men, 41 horses, 44 wagons to week ending 3rd April."
14th May 1852. "A turn-out (strike) of miners (tunnellers) last month

retarded the progress of the Bacup Branch tunnels. Otherwise satisfactory progress. 549 men, 53 horses, 87 wagons."

14th July 1852. "The late wet weather has so materially retarded operations on the Bacup Branch that it will not be possible to run an engine over the line this month, but it should be ready for inspection by 11th August 1852."

These observations were taken for the ELR Works Committee for their minutes 1850 to 1852.

The track was laid with 15 feet lengths of rail, weighing 75 lb/yard. The rails were fastened to chairs spiked down to 9 feet long wooden sleepers placed at a mean distance of 3 feet apart except at rail ends where spacing was closer.

By October 1852 it was possible to travel from Rawtenstall to Bacup and back by train, arriving at the latter town at a single faced platform. There were few novel features, excepting the tunnels, Newchurch No.1 and No.2 and the Bacup Tunnel at Stubbylee. At the end of the latter tunnel nearest to Lee Mill a small platform was made for the convenience of Mr John Holt, the father of J. Maden Holt, whilst a footpath was laid from the station to the drive of Stubbylee Hall. Both the platform and the footpath were a stipulation imposed on the ELR for being allowed to run the line through Mr. John Holt's land.

Increasing traffic by the mid 1850's had prompted the doubling of the line from Stubbins Junction to Rawtenstall. This was completed by July 1857, and so ended single-line working.

Many years passed before the double line between Newchurch and Bacup was attempted, this being authorised on 24th July 1876. The engineering difficulties were formidable and cost prohibitive. The two Newchurch tunnels could not be enlarged to accommodate a double track. John Shay Pering, the LYR engineer, decided to bore a third tunnel parallel to the other two, originally to be known as Newchurch No.3, but from the start earned the sobriquet "The Thrutch". The whole works were beset by problems. On the 9th August 1879, the *Bacup Times* dolefully reported;

"The work in connection with the new railway tunnel at Thrutch, near to Newchurch Station, is proving a matter of a rather tedious and difficult nature. In addition to this, during the past week, there have been a few narrow escapes. On Saturday last, we were informed, some loose dirt fell on four men who were working in the tunnel, but happily they were not seriously injured, only sustaining a few bruises."

As far as Bacup Tunnel was concerned, it was found possible to enlarge it such was the consistency of the substrata. On 30th August 1879, the *Bacup Times* in a more confident manner stated:

"Great Progress is being made on the construction of the double railway line from Bacup to Rawtenstall. One of the most difficult parts of the undertaking was the widening of the tunnel at Stubbylee, Bacup, which goes under the turnpike road between Stacksteads and Britannia, and so is near the residence of Mr. James Maden-Holt MP. On Saturday the Union Jack was seen floating over this part of the new line announcing to the public that the clearing away of the old arch over the single line had been practically completed. It is expected that in the course of the next few weeks the Stubbylee portion of the double line will be quite complete."

But one year later, the double line was still under construction. Not only had there been difficulties with the boring of a new tunnel and the widening of another, but to add insult to injury, the weather did its best to undo the progress. The *Bacup Times* on the 14th August 1880 complained:

"The heavy rains that deluged the Valley during the whole of Saturday had the effect of raising the River Irwell to an unwanted height. Whilst the railway from Rawtenstall to Bacup has been in the course of widening, it has been found necessary to prop up some of the timber bridges by means of large baulks of timber embedded in the river. Seeing the water so high, fears were entertained that the power of the stream should loosen some of the supports and an examination was made which resulted in the discovery that the supports of a bridge at the Waterfoot end of the Thrutch Tunnel had given way sufficiently to make it dangerous for trains to go across. Consequently, orders were given for their stoppage and passengers travelling down the Valley had to leave one train, cross the bridge on foot, and complete their journey in another. Fortunately, a gang of men were soon able to set matters right and now trains are going over the bridge as usual".

During the widening of the line, the intermediate stations at Clough Fold, Newchurch and Stacksteads were altered to conform with double-line standards. Newchurch was renamed 'Waterfoot for Newchurch' in August 1881, Waterfoot now apparently absorbing Newchurch as the dominant place name (Newchurch acquired its name because of its church, built in 1512, the first to be built in Rossendale).

By November 1879, the *Bacup Times*, (as always a font of information about the railway's progress up the Valley) informed its readers:

"A large new station, between the Up and Down lines has been opened at Clough Fold, but the Newchurch and Stacksteads passenger stations have yet to be commenced, though the goods station at Waterfoot is being rapidly pushed forward".

On 28th February 1880, the same newspaper was able to report:

"The new railway station now in the course of erection at Stacksteads is at a short distance down line from the old one. The reason for not rebuilding it on the same site is to prevent the stoppages at the level crossing caused by passenger trains having to remain stationary while the passengers get in and out, thus completely blocking the traffic from Stacksteads to Blackwood. Although the station will be nearer Atherton Holme, the entrance to it will remain as it was previously".

Stacksteads new station was finally opened on 23rd July 1880.

Bacup station was remodelled and enlarged in readiness to take traffic from both the Rawtenstall and Rochdale directions. Originally, the single-faced platform had been accessible from Newchurch Road by archways in the stone wall leading from Spring Street and Manor Street, both means of access eliminated after 1879. The new station became a major news item in the *Bacup Times* for 20th May 1880:

"We understand that an elegant and commodious station house is to be erected at Bacup on the site of the present station and that spacious arrival and departure platforms will be provided in place of the present single platform. The entire work is to be pushed forward with all possible despatch and is estimated to cost upwards of £6000".

It was not until 9th March 1881 that the double line was ready for inspection by the Board of Trade. This was undertaken by the 55 year old Major-General Charles.S. Hutchinson RE.CB. also inspector of the Tay and Forth bridges. The first public service began shortly afterwards on the 17th March 1881 although Bacup station did not officially open until the 27th as it was not completely finished.

The *Bacup Times* was moved to inform its readers on the 4th June 1881 of the near completion of the station:

"The various works at our new station at Bacup are now approaching completion.....Bacup will then be able to boast of one of the neatest stations to be found on the lines of the Lancashire and Yorkshire Railway".

Once in full use, the Rawtenstall to Bacup line had its ups and downs. These were always reported in the local press and today provide a clear picture of railway activities in the Valley.

Bacup Times, 19th July 1884.

"On account of several defects being discovered in the second tunnel at Thrutch on the Up line to Bacup (Newchurch No.2), the Railway Company are making extensive preparations for making it more secure. For some time past it has been anything in but a satisfactory state, especially after heavy rains, the water freely percolating through the roof and falling in large quantities on the line of traffic. Workmen are now erecting scaffolding throughout the tunnel prior to its being lined with brickwork. Traffic, however, has not been suspended although all trains are compelled to traverse the tunnel at reduced speed".

Newchurch No.2 had been lined with blue engineering brick by the ELR in 1852 so that the above account, the observer may refer to relining rather than lining. Also, the Up line ran between Bacup and Rawtenstall so that the reference to the "Up line to Bacup" is a mistake.

Accidents were avidly reported, even minor ones which involved no loss of life. One such occurred at Siddall's Stone Siding at Stacksteads on the 27th September 1884.

"One wagon loaded with stone descended the incline (from the quarry workings), the wire rope broke and the wagon dashed down the metals and crashed into a stone wall. The contents of the wagon spilled on the permanent way just as a 7.50 train from Bacup came into sight. The line was quickly cleared of debris before the train arrived at the spot. It was allowed to proceed normally".

A similar accident was repeated in January 1888, and yet another took place at Bacup on the 17th December 1892.

"Serious accident at the goods yard at Bacup. A shunting locomotive fireman named Brindle (of Bury) jumped off his engine to turn over a 'dummy' and then attempted to jump on again but fell under the wheels, severing his right foot and breaking his left leg and collar bone. He was found by another driver and was conveyed by train travelling from Facit to Bacup, and thence to Bury Infirmary in the guard's ran."

The 'dummy' alluded to was a railwaymen's term for a manually operated point lever.

The public's response to holidays was also observed and reported, perhaps for the benefit of those not fortunate enough to take one. *Bacup Times* 12th April 1890:

"Beautiful weather favoured the Easter holidays this year and as a result the railway traffic was enormous. At Bacup alone, independent of the ordinary traffic, over 2,250 persons booked by special excursions, no fewer than 752 going to Belle Vue on Saturday afternoon. Such pushing, crushing and crowding was probably never seen on Bacup Station platform before and the traffic was so heavy that a special train had to be put on and the officials were quite unequal to the extraordinary demands made upon them. The ordinary passengers to Rochdale were unable to book, and they were compelled to travel without tickets and pay on arrival at their destination...."

The Whitsuntide holidays of June 1897 involved a great deal of coordination between the LYR and local industry, especially as in this year, the holiday coincided with the national Jubilee Holidays celebrating the Diamond Jubilee of Queen Victoria.

Local textile mills closed for a longer than normal length of time. Several excursions were organised by local bigwigs, the so-called "guaranteed excursion" in which the promoter hired a train (or part of one) for an agreed price, made a charge to cover his overheads, and made a profit too! The 'Mount Trip' to Torquay ("the most ambitious venture ever attempted by any local organisation") left Bacup at 10.10 a.m. on the long journey south, to arrive at the resort at 8 a.m. the following morning. Applications for tickets were received from as far afield as Fleetwood, Oldham, Stalybridge, Manchester, Ramsbottom and Todmorden. Seven saloons conveyed the excursionists via Matlock, Derby Cheltenham, Gloucester and Bristol.

The Irwell Terrace Trip ran to Edinburgh and Glasgow, leaving Bacup at midnight and was timed to arrive in Edinburgh at 7 a.m., Glasgow at

8 a.m. Haslingden tradesmen ran a cultural excursion to Oxford, Reading and Windsor, while for the not-so-well-off, there were trips to Blackpool, Morecambe, Southport, Liverpool, North Wales and the Isle of Man courtesy of the Company's steam ships St.Tudno and St.Elvies. Facilities were improved by the railway company at intervals and were duly reported: *Bacup Times*, 7th November 1885:

"Contractors for the work consequent upon the alteration of Rawtenstall Station are engaged in constructing a road from Bury Road to Cow Lane and erecting a wall separating the road from the platform. The platform itself on this side will be extended 60 feet to within 30 feet of the crossing over Bury Road, while on the other side, the platform will be extended up to the gates. A new booking office and parcels office will be erected on the piece of ground now used as a garden by the station master".

The station master's feelings about the loss of his garden was not recorded!

Changes took place in June 1904 at Bacup Station. The LYR converted the terminus into a 'closed' station whereby tickets had to be obtained before entrance to the platform was permitted, whilst ticket collecting at Stacksteads and Britannia on inward trains was abandoned. Gates and barriers were erected and surmounted by two incandescent lamps to illuminate proceedings.

After the establishment of the Rossendale Valley Tramways in 1888, the LYR company operated a service which had to compete for custom. The steam tram was not as quick as the train, but was capable of stopping at more places to pick up or set down passengers. In 1909 the steam-driven tram was replaced by an electrified system which continued to operate until petrol buses took over in April 1932. To combat this literally parallel competition the LYR introduced rail motors in 1906 on an experimental basis although an actual timetabled service did not begin until January 1914.

This service was removed in 1915 as a War economy and reintroduced in 1919, running a longer service between Ramsbottom and Bacup. The *Rossendale Free Press*, 28th June 1919, announced an "...accelerated service between Bacup and Ramsbottom - to be started next week". The announcement continued;

"The Railway Company are evidently bearing in mind the arguments recently placed before them in regard to the need for an improved railway service for Rossendale, and are endeavouring to meet it. They will announce that commencing Tuesday next, they will re-establish the rail motor service between Bacup and Ramsbottom, and for this purpose are putting on 18 motor-trains. Six of these trains will make the journey from Bacup to Ramsbottom (calling at intermediate stations each day except Sunday) and the remaining twelve trains will run between Bacup and Rawtenstall, and occasionally to Ewood Bridge."

The railmotors were replaced in March 1948 by ex-LYR 2-4-2 tank engines, fitted with push-pull gear, operating with one or two carriages. These, in turn, gave way to diesel multiple units in 1956.

Traffic on the line was as the promoters had originally envisaged: scheduled passenger trains, seasonal excursions, along with freight trains bringing coal and raw materials in, and taking finished goods out. In every way, the railway was a boon to the people and industries of the Valley: its demise in December 1966 was equally a great loss.

A Journey from Stubbins Station to Rawtenstall. circa 1935 - The first leg of the railway journey along the Bacup Branch began at Stubbins Junction, the parting of the two routes occurring actually on the bridge over Stubbins Lane. Stubbins station opened on 1st Jan 1847 and found itself short of space between the slope of an embankment on the east and the Accrington Extension line to the west. There were two long platforms, the Up side one the longer and the one adjoining the two-storey station building, comprised of a booking office, hall, porters' room, ladies waiting room and toilets. Access to the station was made via the booking office or by alongside the wing wall of the bridge. The Down platform had no buildings owing to its narrowness. Two unusual features included the lengthened platform which was higher than the old platform in front of the station buildings; the other was the subway at the far end of the station which allowed transit from either platform. The narrow subway still exists, built from dressed stone and white glazed bricks underneath the trackbed, the latter carried on cast iron metal bearers. The near view from the station included Stubbins Paper Mills (now Fort Sterling); Cuba & Union Mills (now an industrial estate) and the Ramsbottom/Stubbins gas works.

Beyond the station, the Branch line appeared to fall below the Accrington line. One writer (Barry Worthington) maintained that the sense of travelling downhill was an optical illusion since the Branch line remained level for a short distance and then rose at a gradient of 1 in 132. Meanwhile the main line also climbed away from Stubbins at 1 in 78.

To the left, the Irwell neared the railway in one of its great meanders, whilst on the flood plain the village of Chatterton complete with brick mill, St Philips Church and rows of stone & brick cottages could be seen. The line now curved away from the main line and crossed Strongstry Road a large recreation ground appearing between the river and the north end of Chatterton. Once again the Irwell swung away from the railway only to return again to force the Branch to cross it by means of an LYR steel bridge. To the left, the main line passed over the Alderbottom Viaduct, glimpsed before the Branch plunged into Alderbottom Cutting.

Once through the cutting, the Branch veered away from the main line completely, the Irwell here 'trapped' between the two lines, the main line carried over the river by the elegant stone Lumb viaduct. (9 arches built 1892). The Branch now continued on a shallow embankment in a north-easterly direction on a rising gradient of 1 in 264. Beyond Lumb bridge, between the running line and the river, were Irwell Vale Sidings. These were situated on the Down side and consisted of two loops and three dead-end sidings which terminated at Irwell Vale signal box (LYR brick 1878). A siding connection permitted access to the sidings from the up line several yards from the level crossing. A shunting neck extended beyond the subway, the latter connecting Hardsough Road to Irwell Vale hamlet on the Down side.

The mills which gave Irwell Vale its name appeared on the west whilst nearer still the river passed beneath Irwell Vale Bridge before once again approaching the Branch. The railway again crossed the river and continued on an embankment across the flat land occupied by the Haslingden, Rawtenstall & Bacup Corporation Sewerage Works, an extensive area of sludge tanks and filter beds which are still there. Yet again bridging the river, the Branch continued in a shallow cutting and approached Ewood Bridge and Edenfield Station. (Edenfield was added after 1890). The little station was 6 miles from Bury and possessed a road-level booking office and sets of steps which let down to both platforms. An open footbridge connected the platforms at the road bridge end. Over the years, the station hardly changed, Harrison and Sale referred to "a flight of steps which descend to the station" from the Haslingden to Edenfield Turnpike. In a relatively recent description, R.T.L. Rees observed:

> "The windows are square, the stonework massive and well-worked. The style, if anything could be a copy of the LYR wooden style in stone, even providing accommodation for the station master in the station buildings." *Industrial Archeology Vol 6 No 3 1969.*

The Up platform was the longer of the two and extended a short distance under the road bridge. Ewood Bridge signal box (LYR brick 1878) stood at the northern end of the Up platform. Near the station, there had been a compact goods yard which consisted of five dead-end sid-

ings, one of which passed through a wooden goods shed with a slate roof, the building being a replacement of an earlier stone warehouse which stood closer to the Down running line. Tom Wray, writing about the uniqueness of this shed, commented:

> "There can be few instances where a stone-built goods shed was replaced by a timber structure. The original shed stood inconveniently at the end of a siding close to the station platform whereas the new shed had a run-through facility and was slightly longer" *The Bacup Branch* 1985.

Extensions to the shed, which were projected by the LYR, never materialised, but the rather dilapidated grey structure still stands today, unusual and neglected.

On a rising gradient of 1 in 150, the Branch continued on a shallow embankment, crossed two occupation bridges and curved towards Holme Mill and Horncliffe Siding. Once more the Irwell bent towards the railway almost touching it, but the main interest lay in Horncliffe Siding. Here, a rough track could be seen ascending the hillside, marking the site of an inclined 3 foot gauge railway which left Horncliffe Sidings and ran under Bury Road. This system belonged to Walton Brothers of Horncliffe Quarries (Rawtenstall Stone Quarry Co. post 1900) who operated the quarry with two or three narrow gauge engines. Thus Horncliffe Siding was a private standard gauge siding for the purpose of interchange of stone brought down from the quarry to the Branch line. Horncliffe Quarries ceased to operate in 1905, the sidings becoming unused. On the Down side, opposite the interchange sidings, once stood the second (1921) Horncliffe Siding signal box, an LYR wood cabin closed in 1929, removed 1936 to Molyneux Jct.

The line continued, still curving north eastwards and approached Townsend Fold where two dead-end sidings were situated on the Down side south of the level crossing and these were linked to the Down line by a single line which crossed the level crossing and then rejoined the Down line. Townsend Fold signal box (LYR brick 1878) stood on the Up side close to the bridge carrying the railway over Holme Lane.

It was at Townsend Fold that a serious accident took place in August 1977 when Class 40 No.40027 hauling sixteen loaded coal hoppers to Rawtenstall coal concentration yard, ran into a car which was on the level crossing, causing one fatality. The *Rossendale Free Press* 6th August 1977 attempted to explain why the accident occurred:

> "The crossing has two gates - one to halt traffic on either side of the crossing. The gate on the Bury Road side of the crossing was in the process of being replaced and apparently had been tied back in a way that left both road and rail open".

A subsequent enquiry found negligence on the part of the locomotive driver and the crossing-keeper, the former failing to stop and the latter failing to carry out emergency procedures.

A short distance beyond, the Branch passed through a short, rock-sided cutting near New Hall Hey, the cutting itself spanned by a footbridge which carried a footpath leading from Bury Road to New Hall Hey Mills. After the cutting, the line crossed the Irwell for the last time before reaching Rawtenstall. On either side were the large-scale New Hall Hey Mills. Only the refurbished (1989) Hardman's Mill is still standing, now functioning as a business centre and listed as a Grade 2 building. Its tall square stone chimney resting on a stone plinth, tapers to an ornate top, a landmark for miles around. At this point there was a level crossing (there still is) where New Hall Hey Road crossed the railway, the crossing gates controlled by Rawtenstall West signal box. The original LYR box (LYR brick 1878) had a slate roof and a brick base. For the benefit of pedestrians, a subway passed beneath the railway just short of the level crossing. The area to the west was occupied by two mill reservoirs whilst to the east an extensive area of sidings could be seen on the approach to Rawtenstall station. The bulk of the sidings lay on the eastern side, adjacent to New Hall Hey Road, in the area now occupied partly by Kwiksave Superstore. At Rawtenstall, the second leg of the Branch line began....

(above) **Stubbins station from Stubbins Lane, 5th July 1964. The ELR origin of the station can be seen in the arched windows. Access to the Down platform from Stubbins Lane could be made by ascending a set of stone steps which ran alongside the west wall of the station building. The lower floor was actually below rail level and was probably used for storage.** *E.Blakey, LYR Soc. coll.*

(left) **An undated photograph showing the western aspect of Stubbins Lane bridge with a headroom of 14' 9", the local council controlled road traffic by channelling vehicles into the centre of the road and by erecting traffic lights. Although too dark to be seen here, the intrados of the arch shows an effective use of skew masonry. The metal girder above the arch overhangs the left-had side, and is supported by a sturdy metal bracket attached to the spandrel. This overhang was necessary to permit sufficient space for the main line to Accrington which diverges at this point. A note for modellers: the roadway under the bridge is subject to flooding and in order to protect the traffic light control cabinet, the council built a small bund wall around it and so that rain did not in turn flood the space created by the bund, a corrugated shelter was erected over the whole thing, seen here on the right of the picture.** *LYR Soc. coll.*

(left) **Stubbins station looking south. This is the actual junction of the Accrington, Colne Extension Railway and the Bacup Branch, the latter leading off to the left of the picture. The cameraman was standing at the end of the Down platform, the wooden fence separating it from the Up Accrington line seen between the converging lines. In the distance, beyond the bridge, is Stubbins Junction signal box, opened in 1900 and closed in April 1968.** *LYR Soc. coll.*

Stubbins station looking north on 5th July 1964. As seen in the previous photograph, the low-level platform has been fenced off and the edging stones removed. Note the position of the Down platform and its narrowness. A diesel multiple unit has just entered the station, bound for Bury or Manchester. *E.Blakey, LYR Soc. coll.*

Ewood Bridge station looking south. Entrance to the station could be made through the gabled building overlooking the bridge parapet. Internal stairs led down to the Up platform whilst an open lattice footbridge enabled passage to the Down platform. Both platforms extended beyond the bridge. The curious wooden cabin perched on the gents urinal escapes explanation but was probably an indoor! toilet for the accomodation on the top floor. *LYR Soc. coll.*

Ewood Bridge station from the footbridge. The mile post, extreme left, indicates 6¼ miles from Bury whilst the 'way out' sign reveals that a separate access was available from the Down platform. The brick shelter (quite a modern amenity) bears an LMS advert showing overnight sea passage to Ireland. *LYR Soc. coll.*

(above) Ewood Bridge and Edenfield station (to give its full title) frontage and entrance on Blackburn Road. The entrance was to the right of the window in an adjoining nondescript stone building which simply covered the stairs down to the station platforms. *LYR Soc. coll.*

(left) Ewood Bridge signal box, fully functional in the 1950's. The box opened in 1878 on the Up side and at the end of the station platform acquiring a new top in 1928, to LNWR type 5 design, on the existing brick base, plus an LYR 16 lever frame. Thus the box was something of a hybrid, officially closing in July 1962. *LYR Soc. coll.*

The rear elevation of Ewood Bridge goods shed, early 1960's. The all-timber construction replaced an early stone-built shed which was nearer the Down platform. To replace with a timber shed was something unusual though somewhat cheaper than stone built examples. An extension to the new shed at the Rawtenstall end was planned but never built. A single siding ran through the shed (note the half-height door) and a small crane, mounted on a loading dock on the other side of the building, could be used to transfer goods from rail to road and vice versa. The goods office was built as proposed on plans dated October 1897. The building is still extant albeit with a lean to one side. One member of the ELRPS has suggested that the Society should purchase the property and resurrect it before it succumbs to wood rot and high winds. *LYR Soc. coll.*

The southern approach to Rawtenstall station in LYR days. The tall signal post marks the position of the final bridge over the Irwell before the line reached the town. To the left stands the stone New Hall Hey Mill with its characteristic lofty square chimney, and the roof tops of the terraced houses which made up New Hall Hey. Behind the foliage, on the right, is part of New Hall Hey Cotton Mill. The photograph was taken from a footbridge which spanned the line at the location of a cutting. *Lancashire Libraries.*

A track-level view of the level crossing and the 1878 vintage signal box, Rawtenstall West, 9th January 1957. The LYR box seen here was replaced by a new box about 9 yards further east on the Down side, this being opened in December 1957 as a BR (LMR) type brick box. The road crossing ran at an oblique angle over the railway so that the gates were off-set. This crossing was not always open to road traffic: the hours of opening of the box were between 5.40 a.m. and 10.00.p.m., Monday to Saturday. It was closed Sundays. *Author's coll.*

(below) **Bridge No.15**, the subway taking the setted path between the two New Hall Hey Mills. This photograph shows the new pre-cast concrete beam constructed in 1956. *(right)* The view at the other end. The date is 9th January 1957.

Rawtenstall in the 1950's. 2-4-2T 50647 stands at the Down platform with its single coach on a push/pull service to Bacup. The canopy, over the Up side, extended from the station buildings, was of singularly plain design leaving the platform free from supporting columns. The arched windows and doorways, so typical of ELR practice, can be readily discerned on the platform side of the building. The building on the Down platform are of L&Y vintage and were erected during the 1890's, the smaller low profile section to the right of the locomotive about 1890, whilst the higher ridge and furrow section, above the coach, towards the end of the decade. Immediately behind the coach we can see a small wooden ground frame dating from 1906 and standing on the site of an earlier signal cabin; the ground frame, of 10 levers, was bolt-locked from Rawtenstall East box at the opposite end of the station on the Down side. The position of the Up signal post gave better sighting for drivers on entering the station from Bacup. Notice that the staff here, like those at Summerseat, took pride in their platform flower beds. *W.A.Camwell.*

Undated view of Rawtenstall station, Up platform buildings at the western end of the station. The influence of the ELR can be clearly seen in the round-topped windows with heavy stone sills, the overhanging eaves at the gable end, and the gas mantle which illuminated the approach to the urinals on those dark nights in winter. The gas light over the small door canopy seems superfluous, the canopy most probably having been added later than the means of illumination. *F.Collinge coll.*

A sign of the past: a wagon turntable situated in the Up bay platform, adjacent to the one-time cattle pens. The table permitted access to the goods shed and sidings and vice versa. Date: 13th June 1964. *E.Blakey, LYR Soc. coll.*

Rawtenstall goods shed, 13th June 1964, bereft of rail connection and awaiting a decision as to its eventual fate. The west elevation with three sets of windows, two loading doors and crane hoist canopy, faced the station yard and the Up-side station buildings. The end elevation comprised a lofty gable end with adjoining lower end wall marked by the ridge and trough roof profile. The wooden sliding doors appear to have been a later addition: notice how the door runner lies lower than the original arch on the right. Look for the firebell attached to the end wall on the left! *E.Blakey, LYR Soc. coll.*

(below) View of Rawtenstall station footbridge under construction in November 1951. *Author's coll.*

(below right) A view of the footbridge on the down side of the station, taken from Captain Fold. Work is still in progress on the flight of steps. *Author's coll.*

A Journey from Rawtenstall to Bacup circa 1935

The second leg of the journey would have taken approximately 20 minutes, and would have passed through fascinating locations along the 4½mile stretch of line. To begin with, Rawtenstall station was different - unlike other E.L.R. stations in the area, it had the distinction of being designed by Manchester-based architects Messrs Holden who had been responsible for Bolton Street station.

Most of the station facilities were located on the Up line side of the station, this part being erected first to serve the single line from Ramsbottom. The single storey stone walled and slate roofed buildings consisted of waiting rooms, goods offices, inspector's office and the station mater's house, whilst below, not generally seen by the public, were storage cellars. A simple flat canopy without the usual valence projected out from the buildings affording some protection from the elements the remainder of the flagged platform uncovered. In contrast, the Down platform, which was built in stages from when the line was doubled in 1857, consisted of fewer facilities and yet boasted both a simple straight canopy projecting out from the original wooden building, and a later glazed ridge and furrow, valenced canopy continuing the platform projection westwards. The Up platform was longer than the Down platform by about 208 feet; standing at the level crossing end, the platforms had a gentle curve to the left. Connecting the platforms was a wrought iron footbridge which spanned the tracks at the eastern end of the station; gas lamps provided the station illumination. Flanking the Up-side buildings lay the setted station yard with a group of cattle pens lying adjacent to a short bay at the end of the Up station buildings. Facing the yard was the original substantial 3 storey stone goods shed with gable end walls and a lower M-gable extension which had its side wall along Bury Road and New Hall Hey Road. The extension was added to the original ELR building by the LYR and comprised a one-storey block built of similar stone. The interior today reveals a roof supported by timber trusses resting on eight cast iron columns : it is now used as a car showroom and occupied by J.A.Taylor. The yard entrance was on Bury Road, the first auxiliary building seen on entering the yard was the weigh bridge office.

Immediately on leaving the station the lines crossed the first level crossing at Bury Road, the crossing controlled by Rawtenstall East Box, an ex-LYR (1880) brick-based structure containing a 28 lever frame. The box was situated in the V-shaped piece of land between the railway and Bury Road. The lines then crossed the River Irwell for the first time on the journey on the Valley route. To the right stood the imposing stone Longholme Mill (felt carpet) which had its own sidings (Longholme Sidings), a set of sidings between the main running lines and Longholme Mill Reservoir (today an ASDA store and car park occupy this site). A further single siding lay between the river, now on the left, and the equally imposing stone built Longholme Shed (cotton) - now occupied by a D-I-Y superstore. Then followed the Rossendale Tramway/Bus depot facing Markross Street. A line of terraced houses on Cape Street could be seen on the left, over-shadowed by the gaunt Ilex Mill (slippers) with its tall octagonal chimney perched on a robust stone block foundation. Ilex Siding just had enough space between the river and the mill, and ran through an arched opening to a dead end. The other end connected the Down line beyond Fall Barn Bridge. It was at this bridge that Ilex Hall Carr signal box stood on timber legs, the cast iron feet embedded in the river. The box was of all timber construction, opened in 1880, and possessed a 24 lever frame. Today, it is possible to see two of the cast iron feet in the river, the timber still embraced in the cast iron, by peering over the wall on Bocholt Way. The railway recrossed the river and was itself spanned by a footbridge which linked Fall Barn Road and Ilex Mill yard. The unusual feature of this river crossing was that the railway bridge spanned the river at an oblique angle and upon the bridge itself the level crossing existed between a private road (leading to Langholme Mill) and Ilex Mill yard.

To add to the complexity of the engineering, a curved weir had been built across the river and a sluice gate which at one time allowed water to flow down a lengthy goyt to feed Longholme Mill reservoir.

A further short siding on the Up side branched off a looped siding, opposite Albion Mill, the siding running parallel to the Up line as far as the gas works footbridge. Hall Carr Mill could be seen to the right across the river, along with a long terrace of houses - Alma Cottages. Our journey has already reached Clough Fold, "The Scented City", so-called because of the all-pervading gaseous aroma associated with the gas works. As well as the latter, there were three gas holders - two on the south side, and one large one on the north side of the railway. The gas works which produced town gas (coal gas), had its own sidings which ran off the Up line at the station. Here could be found the works' shunter, a Hudswell Clarke 0-4-0 saddle tank, No.699, and known as ROSSENDALE.

Once more the Irwell could be seen on the right and positioned between the Up line and the river were River Yard Sidings, consisting of two looped roads and single dead-end road. Here too was Hareholme Level Crossing signal box (LYR wood 1880) located on the down side, 127 yards from Clough Fold station. The box controlled movements at the level crossing which gave access to River Yard Sidings only.

Union Mill signal box controlled connections from the sidings to the main line; a small brick box of LYR 1880 origin located on the Up side directly opposite Union Mill (cotton) which had its own short siding on the Down side. Between Union Mill and Myrtle Grove Mill (wool), also on the Down side, the railway ran along Hareholme Viaduct, a single arch spanning the Irwell. This nine-arch stone viaduct has apparently been overlooked in previous surveys of the line and yet deserves some attention. On close inspection, the following dimensions were ascertained: overall length 330 feet; track bed width 26 feet; height above rive 26 feet; height of arch 20 feet and arch span 30 feet. The arches are lined with five layers of brick, the lining skewed to provide strength. Close scrutiny of the parapet revealed a crudely engraved set of initials, "TW 7 July 1880".

From the viaduct, the brick electricity works could be seen to the left, its high wall rising directly from the river bank. This building is now occupied by Webro Products Ltd, the clue to its former use being at the front on the main road. At the far end of Hareholme Viaduct the railway ran across Highfield Road as an occupation level crossing: the only surviving remnant of this crossing is a kissing gate on the Up side. Once beyond Lench Road overbridge the railway gently curved to the left, once more crossing the river, before entering the spacious goods yard at Waterfoot. With two main running lines and several sidings on either side, this short section of the route probably represented the most complex layout since leaving Rawtenstall. On the left was the biscuit-coloured LYR goods warehouse, built when Waterfoot goods yard was relocated from its original cramped site on the Bacup side of Waterfoot station. The 3-storey warehouse, with its lofty gabled roof, measured about 218 ft x 57 ft and dominated the yard; the sidings were dead end and could only be entered at left from the Hareholme side, all controlled by Waterfoot Signal box (1909), a brick box of 44 levers situated on the Up side near Warth Mill. Today, the old goods warehouse looks as sturdy as ever, now occupied and modified by TNT road haulage company which has taken advantage of a fine building.

Beyond Stansfield Road underbridge, a short dead end siding ran parallel to Warth Old Road - Hargreaves Siding - whilst the running lines and the long siding on the right crossed the river before entering Waterfoot for Newchurch station and Waterfoot Coal Yard respectively. The station consisted of an island platform placed amid the sidings and the Up line. A further platform with imposing station buildings faced the Down line, and was accessible from Bacup Road, a subway joining both platforms. Extending from the down side buildings, was a glazed, eight ridge and furrow canopy, supported on nine iron columns. On the Up side, stone buildings mounted the island platform plainer in design, with hipped slated roof and hipped overhanging canopy. The platform surface was paved with flags except for the ramps at either end which were of timber. P.T.L. Rees described the station as he saw it in 1966:

> "The line runs parallel to the main road at this point about 20 feet above it. Consequently, the station is built on two levels, the lower giving access to the village through an opening that is all too easily mistaken for a shop door. At the lower level, the booking and parcels office open on to the entrance hall which leads directly to the staircase up to the platforms." *Industrial Archeology Vol 6 No 3.*

It was at this station that one native of Waterfoot recalled that long excursion trains would draw in to allow three carriages at a time to be filled (or emptied), before pulling forward so that the next three could likewise be patronised.

Waterfoot coal yard could be approached along a sloping and setted roadway to the east of the sidings, the roadway ultimately leading to Bridge End Foundry.

The setted yard consisted of three coal sidings which were at a lower level than the main running lines. Each siding had its own designation according to its position and other characteristics: "Long Run", the longest siding nearest the Up line; "Middle Run", a siding which terminated near the weigh bridge; and "River Run", a short siding near to the Irwell. Once, these sidings would have been filled with wagons awaiting unloading (or loading) by yard men. Summer and winter, the yard men shovelled coal from the wagons on to waiting horse-drawn carts and the occasional lorry. It was not an easy job, especially during the cold and wet, dark days of winter, when the shovel caught and jammed against the uneven floor of the oldest wooden wagons. Steel mineral wagons were better since their floors were relatively smooth. Today, in the place of wagons, there are mounds of coal from diverse sources such as South Wales and Vietnam! No sidings are visible but amongst the heaps of coal, three ramshackle coal-loading platforms, complete with balance weigh machine and operators dressed in coal-blackened clothes and heavy boots. Deliveries are made in bulk lorry loads whilst local coal lorries line up for their load of coal in one hundred weight sacks.

The railway now approached The Glen and the Newchurch and Thrutch Tunnels. Before entering Newchurch No.1 Tunnel, the Irwell (now much narrower) was crossed again. Newchurch No.1 Tunnel was 162 yards long: before passage into No.2 Tunnel, daylight was restored for a brief time. This spell of daylight marked the short gap between the tunnels. (From the main road, a contractor's transverse adit can be seen in the rock face, appearing as a squat blue-brick portal. It is assumed that the adit connected to the Thrutch Tunnel (592 yards) during its construction.) A backward glance at the Thrutch Tunnel portal was possible as the train left Newchurch No.2 Tunnel (290 yards). Close inspection of both portals today reveals Roman numerals which were chiselled into the voussoirs, presumably as an aid to the masons during construction. Brick lining is clearly visible on the tunnel roofs and sides down to within four feet of the track bed. The lower portions on each side of the tunnels stand as rough hewn rock.

Waterbarn Mills (disused) and the river appeared on the right. Although the river is still there, of course, the mill has gone, the site now occupied by Antrobus Plastics. The line then passed beneath Waterbarn Lane bridge whose sheet iron parapets are still intact despite their rusty condition. Broadwood Siding appeared on the right, connected to the Up line and to the Down line by a cross-over. The oblong Rossendale Mill (cotton) appeared on the left (now occupied by Bacup Shoe Co,Ltd) and yet another siding hemmed in a narrow space between Railway Street and the Down line. This was Stacksteads Coal Siding which ran parallel to the Down line as far as Stacksteads station. Broadwood Siding signal box (1880) stood on the Down side with its rear wall facing the southwest corner of Rossendale Mill - a brick box housing a 24 lever frame.

Stacksteads Station was the last one before reaching Bacup. The single island platform spanned the river and supported a plain timber building with a shallow hipped roof bordered by a deep wooden valence. Access to the platform was unusual, this being via subways leading from either side of the platform at the Bacup end, each entrance possessing a set of descending steps to the subway junction, from which a set of ascending steps led up to the platform. These entrances were covered by a glazed canopy with a gabled roof, the subways walled with white-glazed brickwork. Traces of this subway system are still visible (in 1994), representing the only remains of Stacksteads Station. Once again, P.T.L. Rees referred to the only stone structure at Stacksteads being the urinals, "next to which there was a curious building", this being a hut with three sides of timber and iron railings, surrounding a set of steps which descended from platform level "to an unknown quarter of the station." *Industrial Archeology Vol 6 No 3*

Stacksteads signal box (1881) had a brick base and a hipped slated roof - a small box with a 12 lever frame. It controlled the crossing gates, and stood between the Up and Down lines on the Bacup side of the level crossing.

This crossing was formed by the intersection of the railway and a piece of land running between Newchurch Road and Blackwood. The crossing always proved to be a major obstruction to road traffic despite the shift of the platform towards the west when reconstruction took place. The problem involved road traffic turning left or right from Newchurch Road, only to find the land over Blackwood Bridge blocked by vehicles held up behind closed crossing gates.

A short distance further on the line crossed a footpath leading from Moss Row Cottages and Acre Mill to Newchurch Road, and conveniently avoided a sharp elbow of the Irwell. The double track then passed over Far Holme Lane and ran alongside the north wall of Far Holme cotton mill before bridging a lane to Holme Nook and twice bridging the Irwell. Kiln Holme Mill and Olive Mill (both now demolished), stood on flat land between the river and the railway, the latter yet again crossing the river twice between Olive Mill and Lee Mill. A mini-complex of sidings on the Up side marked the position of Siddall's stone cutting works and Holt's Siding to which it was connected. In his book *Railways and Mineral Tramways of Rossendale*, Bernard Roberts describes the standard gauge incline which set off as straight as a die up the hillside to Frost Hole Quarry. Four locomotives served the quarry lines earlier in the century : HARLEQUIN, STRETFORD, FROSTHOLES and STAMFORD being their names, now long since gone.

The 16th railway bridge over the Irwell since leaving Rawtenstall was crossed just beyond Holt's Siding, the next major feature being Bacup Tunnel (114 yards) which passed beneath the northern portion of Stubbylee Park, the railway emerging from a portal just below New Line, a road linking Newchurch Road with Rochdale Road. Beyond the tunnel was an expanse of flat land originally excavated for railway development last century. The dominating feature was the large stone goods shed which stood close to the Down main line, the yard itself possessing a dozen dead-end roads and four yard cranes. (The goods shed was destroyed by fire on the 11th January 1959). The goods yard was confined to an area of land by the river on the north side and by the main running lines to the south.

On the Up side, the sharp curve of the Rochdale line closed in to form the junction of lines almost opposite Bacup Station Junction signal box (LYR brick 1881).

The string of mills accompanying the last stages of the journey stood on the north side of the Up line: New Hey Mill, India Mill and Spring Holme Mill making up the complement. As the station was approached, Bacup's parachute water column was seen at the tail end of the platform. The 4¹/₂ mile journey ended at Bacup's "elegant and commodious" station, to most Bacupians, an unpretentious building for a modest town set in the heart of Rossendale.

A view from the footbridge at Fall Barn, Rawtenstall, looking towards Clough Fold. A Cravens 2-car d.m.u. approaches Rawtenstall under caution on a Bacup to Bury service. The long curving terrace of Alma Cottages and the gas holders of Rossendale Gas Works occupy the centre-right of the photograph. *Lancashire Libraries.*

Ilex Hall Carr Signal box in sad decline, photographed on the 12th February 1969, almost 3 years after closure. This box opened in 1880, as LYR box 352, and had its foundations set in the bed of the River Irwell, on the Down side, west of the level crossing which it controlled. Note how the access steps to the box led up from the track side, an unusual occurrence due to the confined space of the site. I believe that signal boxes had a measure of individuality by virtue of their style, purpose and location. As work places, they were replete with memories - if only signal boxes could talk! This photograph depicts a sad sight and almost a desecration in the eyes of those who love railways. *Tom Wray.*

Fall Barn bridge over the Irwell, Rawtenstall, on the 12th November 1968, now the course of the 'race track' road known as Bocholt Way leading out of the town towards Bacup. The lightweight steel footbridge enabled passage between Hall Carr Mill (on the south side of the railway) and Ilex Mill (left) and Albion Mill, part of which can be seen with its castellated wall. Vehicles crossed the railway between Bacup Road and Fall Barn Crescent, and also Alma Cottages. A scene no longer with us - a reminder of what used to be when Bacup had a railway connection with the outside world. *Tom Wray.*

Clough Fold station looking towards Bacup on 13the June 1964. Beyond the level crossing is Clough Fold signal box, a 24 lever-framed wooden box of LYR vintage. To the right a rake of mineral wagons is lined up on the siding adjacent to the gas holders which faced the station on the south side. Notice the timber board station building, and the end iron truss, one of many which supported the integral platform canopy. The timber/wrought iron structure is thought to have been an entrance to stairs leading below platform level. *E. Blakey, LYR Collection.*

Clough Fold island platform and the eastern aspect of the station building on 26th November 1966. A d.m.u. stands at the Down platform destined for Bacup. The background is dominated by the gas works building and the largest of the three gas holders: this was the 'Scented City' station on a wet winter's day. The Rossendale gas works possessed its own shunting locomotive in the form of a Hudswell Clarke (works No.699 of 1904) outside cylinder 0-4-0 saddletank carrying the name ROSSENDALE. *G. Coltas.*

(above) **Clough Fold signal box stood on the Bacup side of the level crossing, and between the main running lines. the actual road crossing can be discerned in this photograph between the closed main gates and the box. The open swing gates permitted public access to the station platform, the ramp just visible (bottom right). The stone tranship shed, with its ornate bargeboard, slate roof and chimney stack stands to the right, a reminder of the days when Clough Fold was the terminus of a 3ft gauge quarry line serving Brooks & Brooks Limited.** *LYR Society Collection.*

(above right) **The Waterfoot valley of Rossendale looking towards Cribden End from above the western portal of the Thrutch tunnels. The view was sketched by Harry J.Percival, architect, in July 1880 and shows the railway infrastructure as it was before major alterations took place coincident with the doubling of the line between Rawtenstall and Bacup. The 1856 Newchurch station consisted of a covered platform with the station frontage on Bacup Road. The signal box and goods yard with its timber building were to be demolished, the latter becoming the coal yard serving this part of the valley.** *Bacup Nat. History Society.*

(below) **The same vista in the early 20th Century. The double line is now served by Up and Down platforms, the Down line station building still fronting Bacup Road, whilst the coal yard can be seen to be replete with wagons. Apart from the railway infrastructure the reader will notice the density of housing which has filled the valley compared to the previous photograph, and the electric tramcar on Bacup Road.** *LYR Society Collection.*

(above) **Waterfoot Station from the Up platform, 13th June 1964.** Careful study reveals that the glazed, ridge and furrow Down platform canopy was support by a row of nine iron columns whereas the lighter Up platform canopy was integral with the building behind it. *E.Blakey, LYR Society.*

(right) **Waterfoot goods warehouse viewed from the west on the 12th February 1969.** Rail access is now a thing of the past, this part of the yard strewn with building rubble and a mound of local council salt and grit. The fine building was fortunately saved from demolition and continues in a new role today as TNT road haulage depot and warehouse - an ironic twist of fate! *Tom Wray.*

Waterfoot Goods signal box circa 1967, seen here in a sorry state, empty and forlorn. The box opened in July 1900 with an LYR 44 lever frame, thereby replacing the earlier Goods Loop and Goods Yard boxes, both closed in 1900. The square chimney belonged to Warth Mill (Slippers) which stood to the rear of the signal box. *F.Collinge coll.*

(left) The scene in 1993 from the same view-point as the photograph at the bottom of page 72. The railway has long-gone but the coal yard still operates, now covering the one-time railway. Coal is delivered to the yard from far and wide and then bagged and delivered to local domestic and industrial users, again by road. *Author's Collection.*

(below) Newchurch No.1 tunnel portal (left) and Thrutch tunnel portal (right) as seen from the Waterfoot end. Bridge No.34 was the LYR's designation of the short-span metal bridge over the River Irwell immediately in front of the tunnel entrances, the two tunnels having the designation '35'. *LYR Society.*

(bottom) Stacksteads station from Blackwood bridge, 13th June 1964. The station was unusual insofar as it was positioned above the River Irwell which at this point is confined within retaining walls. *E.Blakey, LYR Soc.coll.*

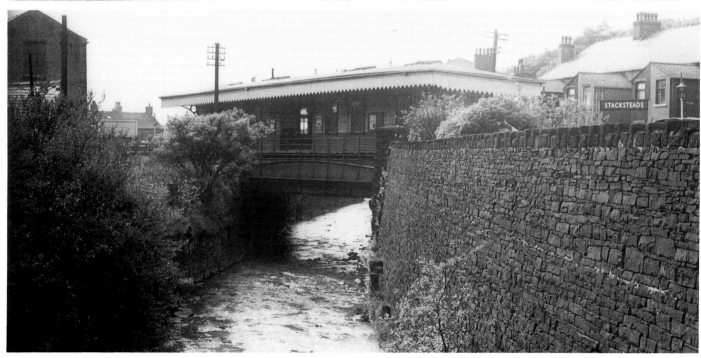

74

(above) **The Bacup end of Stacksteads station, 13th June 1964. Note the setted platform and the half glazed and roofed subway system, one arm passing beneath the signal box and rising up near Blackwood bridge. (The roofed canopy can be seen to the rear of the signal box), the other arm approaching Newchurch Road.** *E.Blakley, LYR Soc. coll.*

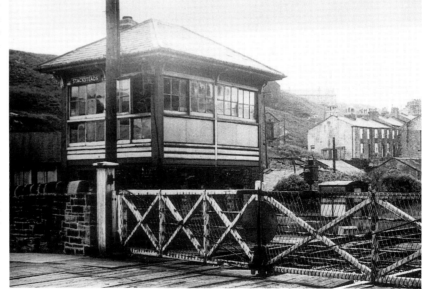

(right) **The Bacup side of Stacksteads station signal box and crossing gates. This box was opened in 1881, receiving a new LYR 12 lever-frame in 1923. Closure took place in December 1966.** *LYR Soc. coll.*

(right) **Twin metal hogsback bridges which carried the Bacup Branch over the Irwell and Lee Road, on the boundary of Stacksteads and Bacup, summer 1993. The bridges are a reminder of what used to be: anyone with a grain of imagination can picture a push-pull train crossing the two spans. From right to left, the train would be heading for Bacup less than a mile distant.** *Author's coll.*

The west end of Bacup tunnel in early LMS days. Ex-LYR 2-4-2 radial tank No.693, of 1898 vintage, sports its LMS number 10927 as it leaves the tunnel on the first stage of its journey to Bury. This loco was withdrawn from service in late 1929. Note the tall signal post and lower quadrant signal arm set off against a white sighting-board. *LYR Soc.*

A few minutes later, the bunker end of a radial tank disappears into the darkness of Bacup tunnel en route to Bacup shed . *LYR Soc.*

Bacup goods yard personnel at sometime in the 1920's. Young and old pause in their labours for a few minutes to have a group photograph taken. Notice the prevalence of cloth caps, waistcoats, neckties and clogs, the daily apparel of men at work as loaders, carters, labourers and the like. *Bacup Nat. History Soc.*

Bacup Goods Shed destroyed by fire. The photograph was taken at 3.15a.m. on the 11th January 1958 as firemen tackle the blaze which appears to be at its height. *Bacup Nat History Soc.*

(right) Ex-LYR 3F 52440 stands with train at Bacup station in the early 1950's. The juxtaposition of the 1st Class slam-door, non-corridor coach and the LMS corridor coach in Bacup carriage sidings add to the nostalgia of the scene. *B.Roberts, J.A.Peden coll.*

(below) The terminus of the Bacup branch - Bacup station platform ramp and handsome balanced bracket signal with Bacup's parachute tank immediately behind, circa 1956. The signal arms controlled departures from the station: the upper arms for routes to Bury, the lower arms to Rochdale. *F.Collinge coll.*

Chapter 6. THE HOLCOMBE BROOK BRANCH

"The station at Holcombe Brook will be near the end of Longsight, and, doubtless in the summer season it will be lively with visitors in quest of mountain air, while the stone quarries at Holcombe will almost certainly yield more of their treasures for the conveyance of which the intended line will be most accessible and convenient."
Bury Times 28th January 1877

The area north-west of Bury, though undulating, rises ever upwards towards Holcombe Moor, and the traveller to Holcombe Brook, the village at the foot of the Moor, has Peel Tower as a focus of his sight. Tottington District; the name of the dominant village being Tottington, an area of farmland, small villages and in the 19th century, having a growing population. the village was not without industry: during that century, cottage textile industry had given way to factory production, carried out in stone-built mills and factories: cotton weaving, cotton finishing, calico printing and bleaching. The main markets for these principal goods were in Bury, Manchester and Bolton, and reliance had long been placed on the far from adequate road network. Just as Bury and the Rossendale Valley had desired a railway to improve communications with the outside world, the Tottington District manufacturers: Samuel Knowles, Edward Mucklow, Richard Olive, Hugh Roberts, to name but a few, subscribed to the idea of a railway, connecting with the main line north of Bury and then penetrating the District thus removing its disadvantage of isolation.

It was a late start, but this was promoted the Bury Tottington District Railway during 1876. An Act of Parliament of 2nd August 1877 authorised the construction of a railway between Tottington and a junction with the LYR line, half a mile north of Bolton Street station. The line, however, did not terminate at Tottington, but was authorised to continue to Holcombe Brook, whilst a secondary feature of the Act was to build a line from Woolfold westwards to serve Richard Olive's Wagon Works. The LYR encouraged the BTDR to act independently. It was a time of national trade depression, of falling receipts on the railways, and a time to reduce expenditure in order to maintain profits. The *Manchester Guardian* of 31st May 1877 announced that the line...

> "would be managed as an independent company, chiefly if not solely, composed of residents in the District, and who, it was expected, would be able to find traffic sufficient to support it."

The BTDR was thus to promote, finance and operate the 3½ mile line

profitably whilst the LYR, whose line it would connect, remained aloof up to a point, yet had some say in the running of the railway. A working agreement gave the LYR 54% of the traffic receipts, in return for the use of LYR motive power and rolling stock.

A notable landowner in the area north of Bury was the Earl of Derby whose estate the railway would pass through. In an effort to protect his land, the Earl attempted to prevent construction at first on the grounds that the railway was unnecessary, and later (1880) that the junction near Chamber House was badly sited and instead the junction should be sited a half mile further north thereby avoiding his estate. This prevarication had little success and the junction at Chamber House was eventually constructed.

The arguments over land purchase continued on and off until 1886, but work began on the first cut on 26th June 1878. Progress was slow: there had been the Earl of Derby's efforts to strangle the line at birth; civil engineering work took a large amount of time up; financial problems occurred with J.M.Smith, the contractor; and the high price of land purchase had to be taken into account. It was contractor Smith who reported in April 1881 that, "there was (sic) 40,000 yards of muck to be shifted" and in July of that year the BTDR engineer informed the Board of Directors that between 10,000 and 11,000 yards of embankment were required at the junction with the LYR's line. In January 1880, landslips had affected the ground at Leeman's Hill, Elton, and at Kirklees, Tottington. On top of this, the purchase of land was higher than at first expected: Messrs Royds sold 7½ acres of land at £600 per acre whilst the Trustees of William Olive required £765 per acre.

Despite the problems, and following inspection by Major Mandarin, the Branch opened on 11th November 1882, without fuss. To allay public fears that the delay in opening was due to an unsafe railway, the *Bury Guardian* announced:

> "We are now enabled to state that it has been arranged to open this railway on Monday next, 6th November 1882. This at once disposes of the innumerable rumours and old wives' tales which have been floating about during the last few weeks. The General Manager of the Lancashire and Yorkshire Company required a little time after the completion of the railway to engage his staff and perfect his arrangements."

Motor fitted ex-LYR 2-4-2T No.50651 working a Bury - Holcombe Brook service in 1951. This engine was the mainstay of the push-pull motive power during the last months of passenger services on the branch. *J.Davenport.*

Although lacking ceremony, the Branch's opening did stir two Tottington manufacturers, Knowles and Roberts, to run employees excursions to the Pleasure Gardens at Belle Vue, Manchester. Normal services commenced on the 6th November with six return trips Bury Bolton Street to Holcombe Brook, with stops at Woolfold, Tottington Station en route, operated by early LYR steam engines.

Back in January 1879, it had been proposed to give the Branch double line status, a status which it never achieved. But the intention had been real as evidenced by the width of Woolfold branch off to Olive's works, and more so by the viaduct at Tottington which spans Scholes Lodge 33 ft above the surface on 9 arches, the piers of which were built for a double track width.

Freight traffic receipts always exceeded those of passenger. The table below provides a comparison between the two from November 1882 to 1884.

6 Nov — 31 Dec	*Passenger receipts*	*Freight receipts*
1882	£244	£277
1883	£1496	£2855
1884	£1352	£2822

Such was the profitability of freight that in 1884, the LYR Traffic Manager, who obviously took a keen interest in the BTDR's fortunes, stated that "there is, as you know, considerable cloth traffic from Holcombe Brook, and it is desirable that the present siding should be extended."
Minutes of the BTDR Company, Jan 1884
Furthermore, one year earlier, the BTDR had proposed to erect a more powerful yard crane at Holcombe Brook to replace the 3$\frac{1}{2}$ ton crane which had become inadequate. At Greenmount, a weigh bridge was to be provided.

Passenger receipts, as can be seen in the table, were always less than those of freight. Even though the Branch might have benefited from the growing popularity of Holcombe Brook as a beauty spot, it had to compete with the LYR's own stations at Ramsbottom and Summerseat which were convenient for reaching Holcombe Brook.

The BTDR's independence was concluded on the 24th July 1888 after just less than six years of operation. From this date, the LYR, which had always been waiting in the wings, took control of the branch by an Act of Parliament of that date.

The railmotor service - From 1883 the BTDR had to compete for custom with steam hauled trams which connected Bury and Tottington. The problem of competition was exacerbated in 1904 with the introduction of Bury Corporation electric trams which travelled over the same route. Clearly, the LYR had to take steps to out-compete the trams and did so by introducing rail motors on its line. The new rail motor car service was given full publicity:

"On and after Monday, July 3rd, the present service of Passenger Trains between Bury and Holcombe Brook will be withdrawn, and in lieu a Steam Motor Car Service will be run at about forty minutes interval between 7.15 a.m. and 10.40 p.m. on weekdays, with an extra late train on Saturday evenings, and a workmen's train each morning in each direction". *LYR ticket advert, 1905*

A Sunday service would consist of eighteen journeys in each direction, replacing the existing service of five. New halts were opened at Woodhill Road, Brandesholme Road Sunny Wood, Footpath Crossing and Knowles' Level Crossing, where passengers could join and alight. The trains were of one class only, but passengers could book 1st, 2nd, 3rd class from any station on the Branch, to stations beyond Bury and vice versa.

By 9th August 1905, the LYR Chairman, George Armytage announced through the *Railway News* that: "We have started running a railmotor

car between Holcombe Brook and Bury, a short line of about four miles. This car has so far carried a considerable number of additional passengers, but it has been running too short a time for use to say exactly what are the financial results."

The first rail motors were of Kerr Stuart & Co. manufacture consisting an articulated unit of steam motor and carriage, the steam motor having the characteristics of two transverse boilers and 3 smokebox doors! These units were underpowered on the steeply graded Branch line and were replaced by Horwich built LYR railmotors of George Hughes design. The Horwich railmotor was more conventional and could be interchanged with different trailers. They were certainly more powerful. As early as 10th February 1906, George Armytage announced:

".....we have built two railmotors, which are running on the Bury-Tottington line, and so far, the results are gratifying. We are building more and I believe we shall find them both useful and economical in those districts for which they are best-suited."

The *Railway News* of 8th July 1905 gave equal publicity to the new Hughes railmotor car service:

"The sides of the car are well-provided with lights over each of which are arranged fan lights opening inwards, affording ample ventilation. Air extractors are also fitted to the roof with hit and miss fittings inside. The seats are of reversible type, covered with canvas rattan, two passengers being seated each side with an aisle down the centre of the car. Brass parcel racks are provided over the side lights. the interior finish is in polished oak, giving a light and clean appearance and the roof is covered with millboard painted white, and gilt-lined on the roof-stocks. Tapestry balanced blinds are fitted above each light. One of the chief features of the car is the design of collapsible steps opposite each doorway which can be let down by means of levers arranged in the vestibule at the trailing end, forming a staircase for passengers from the car to the rail level at the 'halts'; these steps are collapsed together again, before starting, to the width of the footboard. The car is well-lighted by electric light, the current for which is derived from a dynamo driven by a belt from one of the axles: lights are arranged also over each of the sets of collapsible steps, these being switched on at night automatically with the operation of the doors. Steam heaters are of the storage type which derive steam from the engine. Electric bell communication is arranged on the engine and at the trailing end, to ensure proper control of the car, and at the latter end of the car, levers are arranged for communication with the whistle and regulator."

In those days, when the Branch was being used by more commuters into Manchester from the Tottington district dormitory settlements, the style of daily travel offered by the LYR was certainly designed to win back and retain custom.

The Electrification Era - Various lines to the north west of Manchester were ripe for electrification prior to the First World War. The LYR had in mind, three proposals which would establish electrification on: The Holcombe Brook Branch, the so-called Prestwich Line and the Manchester-Oldham-Royton line. In the event, only the former two routes received electrification and for the Holcombe Branch, the impetus came from Dick, Kerr & Co Ltd at the beginning of 1912. The Preston firm had their eyes on an overhead electrification scheme in Brazil and wished to experiment with such a system. The LYR was approached with a proposition whereby Dick Kerr's 3,500v dc experimental scheme could be tried out on the steeply graded Bury to Holcombe Brook route. It was of mutual benefit, since both the LYR and Dick Kerr found the arrangement would be advantageous.

Work on the scheme began at the end of 1912. Gantries supporting the overhead cantenary were positioned between Bolton Street station and

Tottington Junction with single 'tram' masts thereafter placed on the east side of the line. [At Tottington Viaduct, gantries were positioned at either end only, the viaduct itself remaining free from gantries and masts]. A power station at Radcliffe supplied current at 10,000v ac which was stepped down and rectified to 3,500v dc at a substation in Holcombe Brook.

The first fare-paying service began on 29th July 1913. The *Railway News* of 21st February 1914 made note of the pioneering scheme:

"The very interesting experimental line equipped by the Lancashire & Yorkshire Railway for 3,500 volts continuous current, working between Bury and Holcombe Brook, has two motors on its motor coaches permanently in series, and a motor generator for providing current at 100 volts for the auxiliary service of control, brake pump lighting and heating."

And again in the 11th April 1914,

"From Bury to Holcombe Brook, a high-tension direct current system with overhead conductors is now used, creating the unique situation that two radically differing systems of electric traction will be in direct conjunction both introduced by the same company. Traffic on the Bury-Holcombe Brook section is at present worked by a single car, with end and central doors, the latter being provided with steps which can be lowered at stopping places where platforms are not available."

The 'Stopping places' alluded to were at the halts. Brandlesholme Road and Sunny Wood were rebuilt to conventional platform height whilst Knowles Crossing and Woodhill Road were closed from 1st August 1918. Woodhill was reopened in the 1930s.

Despite the incompatibility of the two systems meeting at Bury Bolton Street, the two worked in tandem for at least two known purposes. In order to maintain Holcolme Brook stock, it was necessary to haul it through Bury Bolton Street station and thence to the electric car repair shops at Buckley Wells, there being no overhead catenary south of the station. When, during conversation of the 3,500v system to 1,200v dc, the substation at Holcombe Brook failed, leaving the Branch paralysed. To keep the service going, a third-rail motor car was coupled to a Holcombe Brook motor coach so that 1,200v dc fed into the overhead system could be conveyed to the third-rail car via the pantograph and jumper cables of the Holcombe Brook car. A brainwave solution!

The decision to convert the overhead system to third-rail had been taken as early as July 1913, seemingly well before the overhead system had had time to become part and parcel of the scenery. The conversion process was completed by the early months of 1918, the first third-rail service between Bolton Street and Holcombe Brook starting on the 29th March. The original Holcombe Brook stock was now redundant, its place taken by the third-rail stock. After initial storage at Bury and then Horwich, the LMS rebuilt the four cars to diesel-electric and the complete set put to work between Blackpool Central Station and Lytham, a fitful service which ended in 1929.

Trains Illustrated, July 1951 gave an explicit description of operations on the Holcombe Brook Branch before demise and closure in 1952.

"Tablet and staff operation was in use, with a tablet instrument and non-electrified loop at Woolfold, approximately half-way point of the three-station, three-halt branch, so that two steam goods but no two electric trains could run simultaneously in opposite directions on different sections of line. The guard issued tickets on the train for passengers joining at the halts. Normal electric service consisted of a shuttle service at approximately 45 minute intervals, composed of one motor coach in the morning, plus a trailer from lunch time, whilst on Saturdays three and sometimes five-coach trains. Motive power is now ex-LYR 2-4-2T No.50651, with a two-coach autotrain of a standard driving compartment trailer and an ancient 72 seater LYR coach with longitudial cane-covered seating. Goods trains are limited to two trains down and one up, plus a light engine return working".

(below) **3rd Class Motor Car No.3501, one of 27 ordered in 1914, crosses Tottington Viaduct en route for the Branch's terminus at Holcombe Brook. Note that the overhead catenary was at this point suspended the full length of the viaduct from a gantry positioned at each end, both of which can be seen in this photograph. The chimney framed by the gantry belonged to Tottington Mill. *NRM (Horwich F1261).***

Despite local objections, the Branch closed to passengers on 5th May 1952 after the final steam-hauled passenger train had left Holcombe Brook at 10.26 pm the previous evening. Goods trains continued to use the Branch up to Tottington until 2nd May 1960; total closure was effected by 17th August 1963.

A journey Along the Holcombe Brook Branch circa 1935 - Although the Holcombe Brook service began at Bury Bolton Street station, it was at Tottington Junction, nearly half a mile from Bolton Street that the double junction marked the start of the Branch. The junction was clothed in sidings on either side: Tottington Branch Sidings appeared on the north-east side, accessed from the Up line and fanning out into five dead-end tracks stopping just short of the Irwell. From the outermost track, a further looped siding ran alongside Fernhill Chemical Works which stood in the fork of the junction. On the west side, positioned against Peel Mills, were more sidings accessed from the Down line and consisting of a 'looped' siding serving Peel Mills; three dead-end sidings parallel to the running lines, and two sidings serving the power station on Chamberhall Street.

The general railway infrastucture between Fernhill Chemical works and Peel Mills, lay on a wide embankment, the running lines rising on a gradient of 1 in 400, the double lines reducing to a single line at Tottington Branch Sidings Signal box (LYR brick 1925). Once through the mini-complex of lines, the single line crossed the Irwell on a skewed, five-arch stone viaduct of 303 ft length, a viaduct built by the BTDR for double track, the single track occupying the downstream side of the viaduct deck. [There were actually 6 arches, 5 large spans, and a single narrow span on the Woodhill Road side]. Still curving, the line crossed first an occupation bridge and then approached Woodhill Road Halt. This consisted of a single platform on the Up side, made accessible by a sloping footpath from Woodhill Road. the Halt was positioned on an embankment overlooking 1920's vintage housing in Canterbury Drive and Lichfield Drive, the dominant building being Riverside Engineering Works - now occupied by Winterburn Ltd. Shortly after the Halt, the line passed over a hogsback metal bridge which carried the line over a canal feeder channel [River Irwell to Elton Reservoir]. In its approach to Brandlesholme Road Halt the line ran a short distance in a deep cutting along an upward gradient of 1 in 76 and then 1 in 50. Brandlesholme Road narrowed where it crossed the railway and from the stone parapet, looking west, the second ex-LYR station, Brandlesholme Road Halt, lay in a shallow cutting. The Halt consisted of a single platform and shelter on the Down side, access to which was by means of a set of wooden steps from the south side of Brandlesholme Road.

The line continued in a gentle curve in shallow cuttings with open country to the north east with the large Woolfold Paper Mills to the south west, the line climbing at 1 in 50 and, rising along a short embankment on the approach to the viaduct over Kirklees Brook. A five-arched stone viaduct, 49 ft high, spanned the brook, the line continuing on the other side on another short embankment before entering Woolfold Station, 1.6 miles from Bolton Street. This was the largest intermediate station on the Branch, with two stone-faced platforms served by a passing loop which was the only concession to double track status. The only station building was positioned on the Down side upon which stood a brick booking office and waiting room. The station could be approached from Tottington Road by way of an unnamed lane (now Darlington Close). Woolfold boasted a goods yard which was sited on the south of the station. the 1930 plan shows that the yard had two goods sheds: the one nearest the station had a run-through siding (one of two dead-end sidings) running parallel to the station and running up to buffer stops by the station building. the other four sidings curved away from the Branch, one siding passing through a larger goods shed, and all four ending at buffer stops at the end of the yard. The outermost siding was the longest, the plan showing that it had been intended to continue to Olive's Wagon Works but due to Lord Derby's intervention, it had never been completed. A weighing machine, office and yard crane completed the infrasucture.

On leaving Woolfold, the line passed through open country with fields on either side: Bury Road ran parallel at some distance to the south west, and the meandering Kirklees Brook to the north east. Immediately beyond the station a footpath crossed the line by passing underneath, and a long headshunt ran back to Woolfold sidings. Here, a retaining wall overlooked the headshunt (there were several retaining walls along the Down side on the run up to Sunnywood Halt). Climbing at 1 in 50, the line remained straight for almost a mile before curving south west slightly on reaching Sunnywood Halt. The platform, about 2 miles from Bury, was located on the Down side of the line and possessed a single wooden shelter (sometime later the LMS added a glazed wooden hut). The raison d'etre of Sunnywood Halt lay in the cart track which traversed the line by passing under it, (the cart track running from Bury Road to mills and reservoirs in the valley bottom). From the halt, a large mill lodge could be seen from the platform on the eastern side: to the west were gardens and the rear of houses on Bury Road.

Beyond the halt the line curved north still climbing in a shallow cutting and headed across open country towards Tottington Station. The town football ground appeared on the downside and the terraced houses which faced it on Laurel Street were past as the line bore northwards towards Tottington Station. This was marked by a single Down side platform, 2½ miles from Bury. Close to Kirklees Street underbridge stood a wooden booking office, with slate roof and twin brick chimney stacks, whilst at the platform centre stood a single wooden shelter. Access to the station was made from Royds Street, via a station approach road north of the goods yard. The latter had a simple layout and consisted of a wooden goods shed with a through siding, two dead-end sidings a weigh machine, crane and office. Access to the sidings was by a facing point in the Down direction.

Once under the road bridge, the line assumed a northerly direction, curving a little to the east at first in a shallow cutting, very soon reaching Robert's Siding on the Down side. Originally laid in to serve Stormer Hill Bleach Works (R.K.Roberts) - and since 1903 occupied by Joseph Scholes & Sons Ltd, raisers and finishers, the layout in the thirties was probably the remnant of a larger concern which had undergone several changes over previous decades.

On leaving the siding, the line ran on an embankment and approached the nine-arched stone viaduct which crossed Tottington Reservoirs [also known as Scholes' Reservoirs], the viaduct also known as Bottom Hall Viaduct. The large reservoir, and several smaller ones, appeared on the east and in the near distance the equally large complex of Tottington Mills. Immediately over the reservoir, the viaduct crossed Mill Street, a road which linked the mills to a cross road junction at the town head. From here, on an embankment, the line reached Knowles Siding, accessed by a facing point (in the Down direction), another private siding consisting of two short dead-end tracks and a long curving set of tracks which led to Tottington Mill gas plant. The sidings possessed the usual yard crane and weighing machine both fairly close to the original twin sidings.

Here on, the line ran in a cutting towards Shepherd Street whose crossing of the railway created Knowles Level Crossing the site of the early Knowles Crossing Halt, at 3 miles from Bolton Street. The line continued on an upward gradient of 1 in 50 through cuttings toward Greenmount Station, the station platform being slightly curved and situated on the Down side. There was a substantial booking office on the Bury end of the platform, stone built, slate roof, presenting a wooden facia to the line.

Access to the station was by means of a sloping path which led down from Brandlesholme Road. There was no passing loop here, but a single siding leading back from the station on the Down side at a 15 degree angle to the running line,

Brandlesholme Road crossed the railway on a wooden bridge with stone abutments. It was at this point that the line ascended at 1 in 40 in a cutting and maintained a straight course for about one mile as it headed for Holcombe Brook. The approach to the village was marked by housing which encroached on the railway the nearer the terminus was reached. After this steeply graded approach, the line finally levelled off on nearing the station. In the 1930s, the main running line ran straight alongside the single platform, while a short headshunt and engine release road enabled locomotives to set back to the other end of their train. the station building stood at the end of the Branch.

This was a modest affair, (like everything else on the Branch), standing at right-angles to the line, built of wood with a slate roof and twin chimney stack. Despite its modesty, it accommodated a WC, ladies waiting room, booking office, general waiting room and station master's office. To reach the platform, it was necessary to take a setted roadway which sloped down from the booking office. At the far end of the platform stood Holcombe Brook signal box (Gloucester Wagon Works 1882 design) from which drivers exchanged the electric tablet for single line operation.

Running back on the engine-release road and crossing the main running line gave rail access to the sidings. The goods yard consisted of two lengthy sidings, one leading north to end behind the platform, the other leading south on to a slight embankment. The wooden goods shed and two short coal sidings were also on elevated ground one of the looped sidings passing through the goods shed. The latter was similar to the one at Tottington, having its lower portion on the west side open to the elements. The rest of the yard furniture included two yard cranes, (25 cwt with 8 ft radius and 5 tons with 17 ft radius), one weigh-machine, offices and originally several coal merchants' huts.

Most, if not all of the Holcombe Brook Branch infrastructure has now gone. What is left of note are the viaducts, at Fernhill over the Irwell and at Tottington Reservoirs, where the structure looks as sound as the day it was built. Both can be traversed on foot. Elsewhere, small reminders of the Branch's history survive - there are numerous concrete blocks from which rusted threaded studs project, the original foundations for the overhead catenary masts. At Woodhill Road, an LYR boundary stone is still in situ, now irrelevant, but a reminder of those days when this Company ran its trains to Holcombe Brook.

(above) **This photograph depicts one of the few remaining relics of the overhead catenary system of the Holcombe Brook branch. The four threaded studs emerging from the upper surface of the concrete block originally secured one mast of the overhead line to the ground.**

(left) **Woodhill Road Halt in 1952. Note the timber shelter and the timber-edged platform and the use of cinders for the surface. The electrified third rail was at this time redundant the Branch being worked by steam push-pull train from March 1951. The photograph was taken from the window of the rear coach on the journey to Holcombe brook. *Locofotos*.**

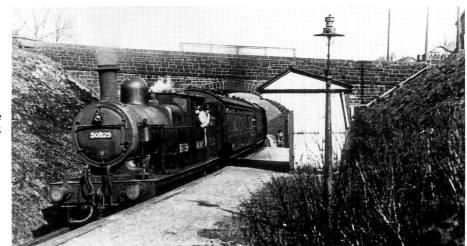

Ex-LYR 2-4-2T No.50829 arrives at Brandlesholme Road halt with the 4.16 p.m. Bury to Holcombe Brook train, 22nd March 1951. *M.Blakemore Collection.*

Woolfold Viaduct looking back towards Brandlesholme Road Halt, 1952. The five-arched stone viaduct spanned Kirklees Brook whose valley formed a deep indent at this point. The third rail is now on the Up side of the line; other photographs show the third rail on the Down side, this alteration being consistent with the Manchester Bury line. *Locofotos.*

Woolfold Viaduct, 30th June 1960. The view is north-eastwards towards Brandlesholme Road and New Throstle Grove Farm which can be discerned amongst a copse. Two landscape machines are busy preparing the ground for new housing development which has begun to creep north of Bury towards the rural delights of Holcombe Brook. *Bury Central Library.*

Woolfold Station 1952. This was the largest station on the Branch and the location of a passing loop. The steep 1 in 50 gradient between Woolfold viaduct and the station can be clearly seen. The notice board on the Up side of the loop reads "Goods Trains Must Stop Here and Pin Down Brakes". Instructions to crew of steam engines were reminded that "Freight trains running to Holcombe Brook with a load of more than seven wagons of coal must be assisted by an engine in rear from Woolfold". Such were the gradients between Woolfold and the terminus. *Locofotos.*

Sunnywood Halt 1952 looking towards Woolfold. Like Woodhill Road Halt, the platform was cindered and had timber edges and faces. Unlike Woodhill Road Halt, Sunnywood's provision for passengers was more substantial, though seen here as dereliction sets in. *Locofotos.*

50731 departs Sunnywood Halt with a train form Bury to Holcombe Brook, 3rd February 1952. *M.Blakemore Collection.*

The south side of Tottington station 1952. The single platform on the Down side has been re-built using pre-cast concrete panels and columns, although the rest of the platform surface consists of cinders and gravel. Notice the gas lamp and the finger post marked 'stop' to which motormen would have drawn their trains up to when stopping at the station. On the Up side of the line, a lone block which supported the mast for the overhead catenary remains a reminder of the pioneering days before 1918. *Locofotos..*

Tottington station and goods yard circa 1951. There was an extensive use of timber for the railway buildings, relieved only by brick and slate for walls and roofs. Note the two posts bearing either a single disc or double disc, a variation of the 'stop' sign for motormen. The large building filling the background was originally an iron foundry on Royds Street South. *LYR Society Collection.*

Tottington viaduct spanning Scholes reservoirs in 1952. The view is towards Tottington station which the train and cameraman had left a few minutes earlier. The viaduct can now be traversed on foot, the old track bed now being part of a linear walkway. *Locofotos.*

The southern approach to Greenmount station 1952. The line at this point was level, a straight stretch of line between gradients of 1 in 50 and 1 in 40 rising beyond Greenmount towards Holcombe Brook. The one-time single siding at Greenmount curved away to the right for a short distance, following the line of the modern fence. *Locofotos.*

Holcombe Brook station signal box in 1952. This LYR all-timber box was opened in 1882, acquiring a LYR 16 lever-frame in 1908. The box became a block box when the Electric Tablet system was introduced for a single line in 1900. The Up and Down "off" indicating that on this day in 1952 the box had been switched out. *Locofotos.*

Ex-LYR Class 2P 2-4-2T No.50829 stands at Holcombe Brook station after arrival with the 2.36 p.m. train from Bury, 24th April 1951. The coaches in the set are 3461 and 24453. Partly hidden by steam above the loco cab is a white cart horse, patiently awaiting the weighing of a load of coal in sacks on the yard weighing machine. The loco crew is engaged in conversation on the platform seat before the return trip to Bury. *H. C. Casserley.*

Close-up view of 50829 with the same train on the 24th April 1951. This loco entered traffic as LYR No.619 on 9th November 1898, built from an 1898 design by Aspinall with larger water tanks and a coal bunker of 4 tons capacity. In 1910, she was rebuilt with a Belpaire boiler, to become LMS No.10829 after 1923. She was withdrawn in April 1958. The leading carriage (LMS No.3461) still carries retractable steps below the door, betraying its origin as a rail motor trailer in use on the Branch before the days of normal height platforms. *H. C. Casserley.*

The 3.00 p.m. push-pull service to Bury about to leave Holcombe Brook, 26th April 1951, an ex-trailer carriage heading the train to Bolton Street. Mid-afternoon patronage appears to be rock-bottom: two people are seated, a schoolboy with cap, blazer and long trousers looks on, whilst the station porter surveys the whole scene from outside the station building. This was quiet, rustic Holcombe Brook before the influx of 'townies' and the increase of semi-detached properties which were to transform the village. *H. C. Casserley.*

Chapter 5. BROADFIELD TO BRADLEY FOLD

"By means of the newly-opened line, not only is there a new direct communication between Manchester and Bury, but the advantages of railway communication are given to the numerous manufactories,and the large manufacturing village of Heap Bridge and Pymhole, lying between Heywood and Bury."
Manchester Guardian 3rd May 1848

The six mile journey between Broadfield and Bradley Fold stations was possible up to closure in October 1970, taking something in the region of 18-25 minutes of normal travelling time. The route the line followed between Broadfield station (394 ft a.s.l) and Bury Knowsley Street station (281 ft a.s.l) was down gradient falling along the slope of land to the Roch valley at Heap Bridge, then falling further to Bury. West of Bury the line climbed away from the Irwell valley and arrived at Bradley Fold Junction before running a short distance down gradient to Bradley Fold station (321 ft a.s.l). The ups and downs of the route being readily seen from a gradient profile. To reduce the effects of the rising ground on either side of Bury and east of Heap Bridge, long cuttings were engineered so that the line spent much of its time within these.

Broadfield station had a somewhat exposed position and before the 1930s, overlooked an expanse of fields to the south (during that decade a large RAF depot was built on those fields now occupied in part by Heywood Industrial Estate), a compact goods yard on the Up side, and a cluster of terraced houses on Pilsworth Road. Access to the station could be made via a sloping path from the road which led to the station approach in front of the station buildings. In turn, to the west, a short distance away, the silent sentinel of Unity Mill chimney overlooked the station, Unity Mill itself being a two-storey brick building with a large engine house and mill entrance facing the railway.

Broadfield station had two platforms connected by a footbridge at the Bury end. The main station building was on the Up platform (Rochdale side), providing a general waiting room, ladies and gents first-class waiting room, booking office, porter's room and lamp room. On the Down side, a waiting room sufficed.

The station must have been a draughty one during inclement weather due to its elevated and exposed position. The prompt arrival of a Rochdale to Bolton train, hauled perhaps by a Bolton or Wigan 2-6-4T, would, in such conditions, have been a welcome occasion......

Immediately over the brick arch bridge crossing Pilsworth Road, the line continued past Unity Mill reservoir and over a footpath subway. The down gradient was at first 1 in 266 and then a steeper 1 in 85 as far as Heap Bridge. The line curved south through a cutting which sliced through open farmland, since developed for housing and industry. A footbridge known as Moss Hall Bridge spanned the cutting and was a focal point of three footpaths which tracked across the open land: from Darn Hill Farm, a continuation of Heap Lane; from Moss Hall Farm, Moss Lane, and another from Bury New

Road (many of the footpaths in the area disappeared when the RAF depot was built but still appeared on maps for security reasons). Beyond the footbridge, the cutting deepened and the line reversed its curvature northwards to become straight at the next occupation bridge, about 700 yards further on (known as 'Bob's Bridge') Moss Hall Road crossed the line on a fine 3 arched stone bridge (Old Hand's Bridge), the masonry roughly skewed as can be seen still on the arch intrados. The subsoil in this area is of glacial sand and clay, the former giving rise to several sand pits such as Prettywood and Boohole. A large indentation in the cutting on the south side marked an old ballast pit. The line remained straight, still confined to a deep cutting and running very close to Spout Bank Farm. Here, another track crossed the railway on a two arched stone bridge, the line now quickly emerging from the cutting as it approached Heap Bridge Junction.

Heap Bridge Junction signal box appeared on the Up side (LYR brick 1900) a structure which was burnt to the ground in a fire in 1971. It is worth pausing here to wander along the Heap Bridge Branch, a minor line in its own right.

The idea of a branch line to serve the growing industries at Heap Bridge had been floated as early as 1860:

> "Industry was developing fast and the growth of the paper works on the banks of the Roch was speeded up by the advent of the railway. In 1860, the LYR asked for estimates to build the line up to Heap Bridge. The cost was to be about £8,000, plans were produced and notice given that the line was to be built." *1846 Before and After* A.J. Dabb.

For twelve years no progress was made owing to contractural problems, but an Act of Parliament dated 24th June 1871 gave the green light and the line was constructed and opened for goods traffic on the 9th September 1874. On completion of the Branch, the *Manchester Evening News* of 30th April 1875 announced,

> "The Lancashire and Yorkshire Railway Company have just completed a branch line from Bury running through the premises of [Heap Bridge Paper Co.Ltd] whereby material is discharged from trucks direct into the mill yard without any carting whatsoever."

One of the Caprotti valve gear equipped Class 5 4-6-0's, No.44745, descends Broadfield Bank towards Heap Bridge Junction with the 4.25 p.m. Rochdale - Southport train on the 15th September 1964. The bridge over the railway in the distance is Moss Hall Road, the new Manchester overspill high-rise flats at Darn Hill dominating the skyline. The photograph was taken from a bridge near Spout Bank Farm.
I. G. Holt.

One of the members of the MBRR and owner of Bridge Hall Mills was Thomas Wrigley who saw the advantages of an extension of the Heap Bridge Branch to serve his works. A siding agreement with the LYR on 21st July 1882 brought the line a further 700 yards beyond Heap Bridge Goods. This incurred further costs since Wrigley had to pay for the erection of a retaining wall, costing in itself £5,000. At the end of the Branch extension, a warehouse was built to receive and store raw materials. From the sidings, by dint of wagon turntables, other sidings entered the works' yard and the works itself by striking away from the sidings at right angles and crossing the Roch on two bridges.

Martin Tillmanns, in his book *Bridge Hall Mills*, described the original scheme as follows:- "The whole network has the appearance of an extremely efficient system. A hundred trucks were used to transport the goods, pulled by two saddle-tank locomotives, popularly known as SAM WELLER and LITTLE KIT".

The 1937 O.S. plan shows that Wrigley's Siding terminated at the warehouse whilst all the works' sidings have been removed. Earlier plans indicate that the main Branch sidings on the eastern side of the river continued past the warehouse to form a U-shaped line (this was on a gradient and <u>may</u> have been to move wagons onto the wagon turntable by gravity one by one) ending in what is thought to be an area for depositing waste material.

In later years, Yates Duxbury (formerly the Heap Bridge Paper Mill, ex-Newbold Bros) possessed their own siding which served both mills. Mill No.1 on the south side of Bury New Road was served by sidings leading directly from Heap Bridge Goods yard (Siding Agreement dated 9th August 1894). Further sidings served the larger No.2 mill, leading back from Wrigley's Siding on the south side of the river (Siding Agreement dated 19th March 1908). Yates Duxbury operated its own motive power in the form of three steam engines which shunted wagons between Mill No.1 and Mill No.2, and down to the junction with the main line. Two were Pecket 0-4-0 saddle tanks; ANNIE (1908) and MAY (1915), the third, an Andrew Barclay 0-4-0 saddle tank of 1904 vintage.

David Mills has commented that,

> "Operation of the system was satisfying to watch due to the sharp curves and steep gradients encountered..... Shunting consisted of distributing the wagons to both portions of the factory and the boiler house from a point adjacent to the bridge under Bury New Road where they left by British Rail locomotive. Empty wagons were returned to this point to be removed later"
> *Bury Transport Museum Journal 1974.*

All in all, the Heap Bridge Branch, its minor complex of sidings and the private extension to serve Wrigley's works, cost in the region of £20,000 for about one mile in length. Among the sidings at Heap Bridge was a stone goods shed with a siding either side of it, and one running in. The building is now occupied by Prettywood Garden Centre and can be easily be seen from Bury New Road. Beyond the old coal yard, the double track singled and passed under the main road through a short tunnel, the portal of which can still be seen; this is a 5-ringed brick arch with a heightened brick parapet standing on the original string course.

After Heap Bridge Junction, the main line continued running straight west, descending at 1 in 263 along a wide embankment overlooking Heap Bridge Sewage Works on the left. The embankment carried the line to meet the "Seven Arches" brick viaduct (1862) over the River Roch (spelt as Roach within the Bury environs) and a further embankment took the line westwards over the tributary Barn Brook. Primrose Hill could be seen to the right (Thomas Openshaw's family home at "Primrose Hall"), closely followed by the end wall of Beech cotton mill. A small area of sidings flanked the Down line on both sides of Gigg Mill Siding which ran at almost 90 degrees to the main line, past

**Fowler 4MT 2-6-4T No.42374 approaches Knowsley Street station passing the sidings between Heywood Street bridge and Market Street bridge sometime in the 1960's. The train was a Rochdale - Southport service, the passengers amply provided for in the four coaches. Notice the fogman's hut and the rod extending from a lever near on the line. Extensive ballasting has taken place on both the main lines and the Bury Loop, in the foreground. A foreign (probably Dutch) van languishes on the far siding. Look for the motor bike and side car left unattended in the sidings. *R. J. Farrell.*

the Lancashire Cotton Corporation's Pilot Mill (1906) and serving Gigg Mills paper works which was situated in the long-gone village of Gigg. A Siding Agreement with the LYR of 22nd November 1898 gave the paper works a connection with the main line. The *Middleton Guardian* of 17th December 1898, reported that:

"The first sod of a new railway siding was cut on Monday, December 12th 1898 at Bury. The contractor, Thomas Wrigley and the engineer Alfred Hopkinson. It will run to the Bury Paper Making Company Ltd and will cross Gigg Lane and an occupation road. The chairman of the directors of B.P.M., John Cronshaw, officiated at the ceremony after which a banquet was held at the Derby Hotel".

On the Up side of the main line, between Beech Mill and Barn Brook, stood LYR signal box No.372, namely Gigg Mill Siding box. This brick box was opened in 1899 and is thought to have closed between 1936 and 1940. Its foundations remain today.

On a falling gradient, the main line to Bury continued in a cutting beneath Alfred Street bridge and immediately met Bury Loop Junction from which a double track kept parallel to the main line as far as Market Street bridge before curving away to the south west, eventually to join the East Lancashire line at Bury Loco Junction. Between Alfred Street and Heywood Street bridges stood Bury Loop Junction signal box, a brick built LYR cabin of 1898. Beyond Heywood Street, in addition to the Loop line, the main line was accompanied by three dead-end sidings their buffer stops positioned at the Heywood Street end. Even more dominant was the array of sidings which fanned out to the right into Knowsley Street goods depot.

Here, there were three goods buildings, numerous yard cranes and a weigh machine to serve the complex of sidings which spread out on the western side of Market Street bridge. Overlooked by the latter stood Knowsley Street East signal box, another LYR brick cabin of 1898.

Four lines passed through Knowsley Street station, the two centre Up and Down roads principally used for goods traffic, but also for excursion passenger traffic to and from the Bolton direction. On running beneath Knowsley Street bridge (1848), Bury East Fork curved away up gradient to enter Bolton Street station at Bury South Junction. The four lines continued a short distance between Knowsley Street bridge and Manchester Road bridge, and at Knowsley Street West signal box (LYR wood 1909), reduced to double track. Here, the lines dipped under the East Lancashire Railway, a dip pronounced enough to earn the official name of "Bury Hollow".

Bridge Road crossed the line, the latter now curving gently south west over a subway bearing a footpath from Tenterden Street to Hardman's in the Fields Farm. Inner Bury had now been left behind and the line entered the district of Elton. To do this, the line had to cross the Irwell on a 140 yard, 5-arch (66 feet span) stone viaduct which carried the railway not only over the river, but also the Manchester, Bolton & Bury Canal and Wellington Street.

The viaduct is worthy of inspection today, demonstrating as it does the art of skew construction in its five arches. The masons' skill is seen in the stone faces which stare down from the plain parapet and from the towers at either end.

This area was dominated by large brick mills, namely, Elton Paper Mills, New Victoria Mills, Wellington Mill, Egyptian Mills (with its octagonal stone chimney) and Daisyfield Mills. Continuing on an embankment, overlooking Railway Terrace, the Bolton line passed a half-moon-shaped reservoir (Crompton's Lodge) and crossed another subway bearing a path from Deardens Street and Milne Street. To the left were the large grounds surrounding the Florence Nightingale Hospital and on the right, a series of sidings for colliery wagons marked the junction with Gas Works Sidings. The junction was controlled by Gas Works Siding signal box (LYR brick 1892), seen on the right-hand side.

As in the case of the Heap Bridge Branch, it is worth pausing here and

LMS 2P 4-4-0 No.40588 gathers speed as it leaves Bury on a Rochdale - Wigan service, 27th March 1960, shrouding the top of the 'off' distant signal in exhaust. Part of Bury Grammar School building and playing fields are seen to the left of the engine's buffer beam. *R. J. Farrell.*

taking a look at the Gas Works Siding (officially known as Bury Corporation Gas Siding). The origin of the siding rests on a Siding Agreement with the LYR dated 10th April 1890. Access/exit was from a trailing point on the down line and then over a single slip point on the up line. A further trailing point on the Up line beyond the signal box permitted access (by reversal) and exit from the sidings on to the Up line only.

The siding was double as far as the 118 yard tunnel beneath Bolton Road and Fountain Street, passing through and emerging as a single line to the gas works. Construction of the sidings were commenced on 19th August 1891 and completed in November 1893, costing initially £39,594. The first supplies of coal arrived on 1st February 1893.

With many siding extensions, the total trackwork amounted to 1½ miles by 1922, enough to warrant the use of two Nasmyth Wilson and Co. 0-4-0 saddle-tank locos, one of which was named ELTON, the other BURY, the former replaced by a Hunslet-Barclay 0-4-0ST shunter sometime later. The Gas Sidings closed about 1959, the tracks were lifted in 1965 after 66 years of service for Bury Corporation.

The line beyond Bury Gas Junction continued in a cutting directly south west, paralleled by two sidings on the Up side which passed under a cast iron bridge on brick abutments. The original road bridge over the main line was a brick arch and together the two adjoining bridges converged the road access to Florence Nightingale Hospital. The line ran into open country, passing St.Stephen's Recreation Ground on the right and farmland on the left. A further occupation bridge crossed the line carrying Coal Pit Lane from Bolton Road and from here on, the line ran straight with farmland on either side, dotted with nearby farmsteads such as Lower Spen Moor, Middle Spen Moor, Higher Spen Moor, Buckley Fold and Round Oak. This part of the route followed a cutting on an upward gradient of 1 in 207 and was crossed by a further three occupation bridges before arriving at Black Lane station, 2 miles and 1 chain from Bury.

The station nestled in a cutting with high retaining walls, surrounded by a compact area of industrial premises on the Bury side of Ainsworth Road. Black Lane Mills (formerly Tootal, Broadhurst Lee Co.Ltd) possessed its own siding (LYR Siding Agreement dated 31.7.1882.) (Agreement with Black Lane Mills dated 8.4.1915) accessed from a turntable positioned on a siding parallel to the Down line. On the Up side, Black Lane Engineering Works (1907), owned by Whittaker Hall & Co.Ltd also overlooked the station. The station itself consisted of two platforms, the Up side holding the main station building, leaving the Down side with fewer facilities. The original station was opened by the Lancashire & Yorkshire Railway on the 20th November 1848 with subsequent alterations by that company.

In August 1927, Black Lane station was the scene of severe flooding following torrential rainfall and the bursting of streams in the area:

> ".... with surprising rapidity, the permanent way was, for 300 yards, flooded. The depth of the water was 3 feet and this was easily observable by the marks on the stonework facing the metals. Traffic was stopped after the train which left at 4.15 and it was necessary to divert (the train) between Bury and Bolton on to the line which branches off at Whittaker Fold Farm.... The flooding of the permanent way was due to the inability of a culvert, which runs underneath it, to take the immense volume of water." *Radcliffe Guardian* 20th August 1927.

Immediately beyond Ainsworth Road bridge, on the Bolton side, stood the tall Black Lane signal box (LYR brick 1913) at the far end of the Up platform. The line continued in a diminishing cutting towards Bradley Fold Junction, paralleled by a long refuge siding on the Up side. Standing at the junction with the line back to Radcliffe was Bradley Fold Junction signal box (LYR brick 1902) positioned on the Down side of the junction. An occupation bridge carrying a road from Moss Shaw Farm crossed the line immediately beyond the junction, and from here, the line curved to a more westerly direction as it approached Bradley Fold station, 3 miles from Bury. Beforehand, on the Down side, stood Bradley Fold East signal box (LYR wood 1908) plus a set of sidings and headshunt leading from a trailing crossover from the Down line.

A Siding Agreement with Dobson & Barlow (dated 6.4.1908) whose sidings they were, permitted access to the works on the Bolton side, and a further connection originally existed at the eastern end of the sidings with the Up line. The 1937 O.S. plan shows the sidings extended to serve the eastern side of the works (by then expanded in size) whilst the eastern connection with the Up line had been removed. Radcliffe Moor Road crossed the line (on a single arched bridge) with large stone voussoirs contrasting with the brick. A short distance from this (200 yards), Bradley Fold station was reached. Like Black Lane station, the location coincided with the crossing of a road, in this case, a level crossing, and where a small community existed, gathered round a cotton mill-Fold Mill. The station was opened by the Liverpool & Bury on 20th November 1848 and was positioned on the eastern side of the road crossing the main station buildings occurring on the Down side, leaving two separate brick buildings on the Up side. The Up side (Bolton to Rochdale) buildings comprised a general waiting room, porter's room, ladies room, with a urinal attached at the far end. The Down side accommodated the same with a booking office.

The platforms were joined by a lattice iron footbridge which also permitted pedestrians to cross the railway when the gates were against road traffic on Tong Road. Before 1888, a footpath had run alongside the level crossing but was found to be somewhat dangerous and about 1890 was abolished, its place taken by a stepped footbridge, bent towards the platforms, its height above rail level being 15 feet.

On the Bolton side of the crossing stood Bradley Fold station signal box (LYR wood 1907) on the Up side, with its back to the Queen's Hotel. Westwards, the main line became four roads, the Up and Down main paralleled by an Up and Down goods loop respectively, for a distance of 1,313 yards. Bradley Fold goods yard was sited on the Down side, consisting of four dead-end sidings, yard crane and station house. Rail access to the yard was from either a trailing crossover from the Up line opposite the signal box (which led to a siding with a headshunt parallel to the Down loop), or from the Down line, 350 yards further west.

As at Radcliffe, plans show that Bradley Fold station and crossing were supported by coal pillars purchased by the LYR from the Earl of Wilton and Trustees, and from Thomas Fletcher & Sons, by an Agreement dated 12th October 1883.

Hughes Cl.6P5F 2-6-0 No.42750 passes Spout Bank Farm on leaving Heap Bridge Junction signal box (in distance). This is the 11.47 a.m. Saturdays only Bolton - Leeds Central train on the 4th November 1961. Note the freshly ballasted tracks. *R. J. Farrell.*

45232 draws a rake of empty steel mineral wagons away from Heap Bridge Junction towards Broadfield on 28th June 1965. Heap Bridge Junction signal box can be seen, framed by the left-hand arch, whilst the bracket signal with sighting board, is 'off' for the train to take the gradient of l in 85 uphill to Broadfield. *R. J. Farrell.*

(right) BR Standard Cl.4 4-6-0 No.75016 takes advantage of the down gradient past Heap Bridge Junction signal box with a Rochdale - Southport train on 4th November 1960. The signal box stood on the V of land between the Up main line and the Heap Bridge Branch, and housed an LYR 20 lever frame. The box met its demise by being burned down in January 1971 and was closed the following March. *R. J. Farrell.*

(opposite) Passing under Moss Hall Road bridge, Kingmoor based Stanier Cl.5 No.44795 heads a Carlisle - Oldham (Glodwick Road) empty van train up the Broadfield Bank on the 8th July 1966. Notice the sighting board arched by the bridge; this would be painted white and facing oncoming traffic to facilitate better visibility. *R. J. Farrell.*

(left) **Roch Valley Rail Society special (reporting number 1Z30) halts at Heap Bridge goods yard, primarily a coal yard in the 1960's, the exact date being 28th July 1962. The two locomotives involved with this train were Aspinall 3F 0-6-0 No.52523 and Fowler 3MT 2-6-2T No.40063. Both had brought the special from Rochdale and were to continue their journey via Knowsley Street station, Bolton Street station and then Tottington to Bacup. Enthusiasts have alighted and wander about the yard which is now part of the car park of the Prettywood Garden Centre the latter occupying the former goods shed. *I.G.Holt.***

(below) **0-4-0ST MAY hauls two sheeted wagons along the branch line which had served Bridge Hall Paper Mills and now served Transparent Paper Ltd. The extension of lines from Heap Bridge goods yard passed alongside TP's premises on the east bank of the river Roch before terminating at a reception warehouse. *R.J.Farrell.***

The Heap Bridge branch trio, two at rest and one in steam, circa 1970. From left to right the locomotives are: ANNIE, a Pecket 0-4-0ST of 1908 vintage; MAY, a Pecket 0-4-0ST of 1915 vintage and an unnamed Andrew Barclay 0-4-0ST, built 1904. The location depicted is thought to be on the straight section of the single line approaching Yates Duxbury's No.2 Mill. *J.A.Peden.*

MAY at work on the sharply curved and inclined single line branch into Yates Duxbury's sidings. The roof of Heap Bridge goods shed can be seen 'above' the white paling fence and the stone retaining wall which supported the ground and Bury Road. The sharp bend of the Roch can be seen extreme right. *R.J.Farrell.*

(below) ANNIE at rest on the 26th August 1967. Industrial loco-buffs will savour the following details: full-length tank, flared wing plates at the front of the smokebox, Ross-pop safety valves mounted on the flattened dome, and like MAY, had her whistle mounted on the cab roof. *J.A.Peden.*

(below) **Andrew Barclay 945/04** in a sylvan setting on the Yates Duxbury branch on the 22nd May 1971. This locomotive had a square-sided, round-topped tank with a tall tapered chimney, filler and Ramsbottom pattern safety valves. The cab had port-hole windows at the front, rear and side, the water tank extending just short of the smokebox door. An unusual feature was the high position of the buffer plates on the buffer beam. *A.J.Cocker.*

(left) **A close view of "Seven Arches" over the River Roach on the 9th July 1966. A diesel multiple unit crosses the viaduct en route to Knowsley Street station on a Rochdale to Bolton service. The piers closest to the river have been erected on stone bases with rounded ends to ease the flow of the river (from left to right). Although disused since the line's closure, the viaduct is in good repair and will once again carry rail traffic on the single line of the ELR from Bolton Street to Heywood..** *R. J. Farrell.*

(opp. top) **Ivatt Cl. 2MT 46416 leaves the Down line of the Bury Loop and is about to cross the Down main. Notice the calling-on signal (just above second tank), allowing the train to draw forward on to the Up main where it will reverse into Knowsley Street sidings. The Up main passed through the arch (right); the Down platform and through lines passed through the middle opening, leaving the Loop lines to make use of the left-hand opening. Date: 22nd April 1965.** *R. J. Farrell.*

(opp. middle) **A busy scene on the approach to Knowsley Street station (in the distance beyond Market Street bridge), seen from Heywood Street bridge, 19th May 1965. P.W. staff pause their work as two Black 5's ease forward, while a freight train occupies the same road at a distance behind. (see table on page 35 for the comings and goings at these sidings) The Bury Loop has already commenced at this point, actually at Bury Loop Junction which is behind the cameraman, and can be seen in this photograph on the extreme left. Note that high-visibility vests were not standard practice in the 1960's for anyone working the railway.** *R. J. Farrell.*

(below) **WD 90366 doubleheaded with Stanier 8F 48102 draw a heavy track laying train, bound for Castleton P.W. depot, past Bury Loop Junction signal box on 21st February 1960. The box was opened in 1898 in connection with Bury Loop and housed an LYR 48 lever frame. After a devastating fire in March 1967 the box was closed. Note the tall lattice signal post, the parachute type water column near Heywood Street bridge and the catch points on the Up road of the Bury Loop positioned to prevent runaway wagons fouling the main Down line.** *R. J. Farrell.*

Another view east from Market Street bridge depicting a scene which was regarded as so common-place in the early 1960's that little was thought of it and few realised that this would be history by 1970. Stanier 8F 48295 hauls a load of coal in 16 ton steel mineral wagons towards Knowsley Street station on 26th April 1965 while Stanier 4MT 42484 appears to wait her turn with a short rake of mixed freight wagons and brake van. *R. J. Farrell.*

(above) Ex-LMS 3F No.47584 takes water on the Bury Loop line near Bury East signal box, 4th December 1959. The driver standing on the tank top seems at a loss possibly as to why the supply of water has not yet reached his engine while his fireman looks on. The overturned brazier grates at the foot of the water column are not yet required to prevent water freezing, whilst the bricked up locking room windows in the rear wall of Bury East box are a result of Second World War bomb-blast prevention, most work of this nature carried out in the years before 1939. Market Street bridge is in the near background. *R. J. Farrell.*

(left) Stanier 4MT 2-6-4T No.42592 leaves Knowsley Street station on 5th March 1960, probably on a Rochdale to Bolton service. The all-timber Bury West signal box was overlooked by Manchester Road bridge, and the set of bracket signals (to the left of the exhaust) controlled the East Fork approach to the station. A 20 m.p.h. speed restriction was in force on the Up main line into the station indicated by the sign to the left of the engine front. Bury Town Hall dominates the view over the bridge. *R. J. Farrell.*

Stanier Black 5 No.45341 takes a down freight of vans out of Bury on the 15th May 1959 bound for Hellifield. Two bridges can be seen in this view, firstly the brick-built Bridge Road underbridge, and behind the metal span bridge bearing the line into Bolton Street station (left). *R.J.Farrell.*

(above) Ex-LNWR 7F 0-8-0 No.49147 makes a rare visit to the Bury area hauling a rake of vans eastbound towards Knowsley Street station, on 30th June 1961. Westbound freight traffic on the Bolton - Rochdale line through Bury had originated in Yorkshire for Lancashire markets, with Moston Sorting Sidings being a common terminus for eastbound traffic. The fifth van has just emerged from under Bridge Road underbridge. Notice the Grammar School tennis court (extreme right) and the cluster of mill chimneys gathered round the Wellington Road area. *I. G. Holt.*

(right) WD 90112 lays down a smokescreen as it hauls a heavy train of loaded mineral hoppers towards Bury on the 3rd February 1960. Left of the engine is the octagonal Egyptian Mill chimney with Daisyfield Mill chimney beyond the mill. *R. J. Farrell.*

(above) BR Class 9F 2-10-0 No.92161 glides effortlessly across the Irwell viaduct at Elton, on 8th February 1960, with a Carlisle - Oldham empty van train towards Knowsley Street station. The viaduct still stands as a testiment to the skill of the early Victorian civil engineers. Unfortunately, the viaduct is not a listed building and if not protected, will slowly deteriorate. *R. J. Farrell.*

(left) Detail of one of the arches of the Irwell Viaduct at Elton. Note the skewed masonry of the intrados (the arch surface) which gave the arch its strength.

(below) LMS 3F 0-6-0T No.47224 runs bunker first back to Bury on a cold 13th January 1960 with a rake of mainly 16 ton steel mineral wagons from Bury Gas Works sidings. The train is approaching the Irwell viaduct which spanned the river, canal and Wellington Road. The locomotive crew are probably huddled inside the cab in an attempt at keeping warm. *R. J. Farrell.*

(above) **44989** passes Bury Gas Works Sidings box on the Bolton side of Bury with the 4.25 p.m. Rochdale - Southport train on 22nd June 1962. In these days of two-car Sprinter-operated Coast to Coast expresses, (Liverpool - Scarborough), a seven coach train of corridor stock seems somewhat extravagant - the Rochdale - Bolton - Liverpool route was to give way to rationalisation by 1970. The Gas Works Siding was accessible from the down line by means of a crossover (a double-slip point exists left of engine) and by reversal from the Up line at trailing points beyond the signal box. *I. G. Holt.*

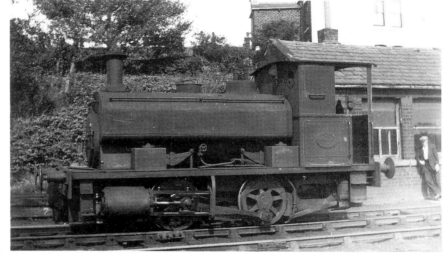

(right) Hunslet - Barclay 0-4-0ST pauses in its shunting duties at Bury Gas Works sidings in August 1957. The engine had a full-length tank, and forward port-hole windows. There was no coal bunker. The exposed rear must have been a nightmare on the foot plate during winter and in driving rain. *Bury Central Library.*

Black Lane signal box on 2nd June 1957. Opened in 1913 as LYR box 377, Black Lane box was located on the Up side, close to Ainsworth Road bridge, and replaced an earlier box which had stood on the end of the Down platform since 1891. The tall box seen here gave the signalman a clear view over the bridge, his view to the west being unrestricted. Access to the working area would have been by internal stairs from a door at track level. The locking-room windows had been bricked up as a pre-war blast damage expediency. *Radcliffe Library.*

(above) **A tidy Black Lane station, Down platform, as seen from Ainsworth Road bridge on 22nd June 1963. The main station buildings occupied space on the Up platform, while a compact timber-sided, hipped roofed waiting room with adjoining urinal sufficed on the Down platform. Note the prevailing gas lamps (still in use despite the age of electricity) and the two-wheeled platform barrow near the rear wall - both part and parcel of the railway scene. The well-kept building in the background is the rear of Black Lane Cotton Mill.** *Radcliffe Library.*

(left) **Radcliffe Black Lane station looking towards Bury and taken from the Down platform beneath the arch of Ainsworth Road bridge in 1964. The platforms were of equal length but slightly staggered so that the down platform extended beyond the bridge towards Bolton. In the distance, close to the Up line, is Whittaker Hall, light engineers, and an occupation bridge which carried a lane from Mill Street to Hardman's Fold.** *Radcliffe Library.*

Stanier Cl.5 No.44803, of Newton Heath, heads the 3.45 p.m. Rochdale - Liverpool through Radcliffe Black Lane 21st July 1962. *Ian G.Holt.*

(middle) Stanier Cl.5 No.44808 approaches Radcliffe Black Lane station with a Morecambe - Shaw relief on 18th August 1962. *Ian G.Holt.*

(bottom right) Bradley Fold Station signal box, 14th June 1958. This all-timber box was opened in 1907 as LYR 380, located in the same place as an earlier (1879) box, that is, on the Up side and west of the level crossing. The neat and tidy appearance was radically disrupted circa 1960 when the bottom half was rebuilt in brick. Note that in contrast to many boxes in the area, the locking room windows are intact, complete with 4 panes of glass in each. Closure took place on 3rd October 1970. *Tom Wray.*

(below) Bradley Fold East signal box, 14th June 1958. This box was narrower than the standard 12 foot width and had opened in 1908 as LYR 379. To the rear of the box are the sidings and northern elevation of Mather & Platt Ltd whilst in front is the Up line to Bradley Fold Junction. The box had 14 working levers and 10 spare, closing on 17th May 1967. *Tom Wray.*

"The Radcliffeites have their full share of Lancashire grit and generosity and inventiveness and wit. They have advantages in being in the neighbourhood of coal mines, and communications by canals and railways, and last, but not least, in touch with the mighty lodestone of Manchester."
The History and Traditions of Radcliffe. Rev.W.Nicholls

Lying three miles to the south-west of Bury, the town of Radcliffe has the privilege of sharing the broad valley of the River Irwell with that of its larger neighbour. Overshadowed by the larger town, Radcliffe is not a place of distinction, there being no equivalent of Sir Robert Peel and John Robinson Kay to highlight its industrial history. Instead, the town has ranked with many others in south east Lancashire's industrial belt closely involved with textiles, paper-making and coal mining. In the latter industry, eleven collieries operated within the parish boundary, in the 19th century: Outwood, Stand Lane, Coney Green, Wilton, Monkey Pit and others were busy extracting the black gold from beneath the town.

There were really two Radcliffes: Radcliffe Bridge, crossing-point and industrial focus, and Radcliffe itself, lying north of the Irwell, at the eastern end of Spring Lane.

A map of this period shows the importance of Radcliffe Bridge approached from the south-west by Stand Lane (part of the Bury and Prestwich Turnpike) and from the north-east by Blackburn Street (a continuation of the same turnpike). In the mid 19th century, coal mines, cotton mills, bleach works, dyeworks, calico printing works were dotted about the parish, all taking advantage of the local resources; coal - coal and soft water.

During this nascent stage of 19th century industrialisation, the two Radcliffe's merged into one, and grew as an industrial town [population 1821:*3,089*; 1841:*5,099*; 1851:*6,293*] and one deemed large enough to possess a railway station at Radcliffe Bridge, close to Sion New Road on the north east side of the river. The 1850 map shows the course of the ELR route from Clifton Junction to Bury, spanning the Irwell (seven miles from Manchester) and skirting the northern outskirts of the town, crossing Sion New Road, and then diving under Blackburn Street and Spring Lane before heading off to Bury.

Harrison and Sale described the early scene around Radcliffe Bridge in their survey of 1846:

"Passing through the deep Outwood Cutting, the line again crosses the Irwell on a timber and stone viaduct (five openings, 55 feet span), 75 feet above the river and soon reaches Radcliffe Bridge, a busy and populous manufacturing village, (created by the judicious tenure of land from the Earl of Wilton), which spreads its manufacturing establishments over a large space of ground to the right of the line."

How different the map looked by 1890, for then Radcliffe had expanded in size (population 1891: 24,972), replete with houses, factories and mills, and now a veritable crossroads of railways. Like Bury, Radcliffe too had a non-planar intersection of railways, where the 1879 line to Bolton passed over the ELR line to Bury on the northern edge of the town.

Between November 1881 and November 1890 agreements were made between the LYR company, Messrs A.Knowles and Sons Ltd, and the Earl of Wilton and Trustees whereby pillars of coal were to be left in situ underground so preventing land subsidence due to mining. A study of plans drawn up shows the disposition of the supporting pillars which were deliberately left in the '2 yard' or '6 feet Mine' which underlay the town. Radcliffe New Station (Central), the goods yard, Radcliffe Viaduct (1879), Hagside Bridge, West Junction Bridge and Spring Lane stand above these supports, the whole area beneath the town being riddled with galleries which followed the 2 yard seam.

Having set the general scene, let us progress forward and trace the history and events of each strand of Radcliffe's railways, and then describe the routes which pass through the town as it was in LMS days.......
To begin with, it is worth mentioning a railway of which little has been made public knowledge. This was a private affair instigated and owned by A.C. Bealey & Sons, bleachers and dyers, whose works stood on Dumers Lane. In the early years of the 19th century, one of the main raw materials was rock salt and this had to be brought into Radcliffe by canal barges as far as Hagside Wharf on the Manchester, Bolton & Bury Canal. From the wharf, horse-drawn carts carried the commodity to the works. About 1850, the firm laid a single line standard gauge railway from the works' yard to Hagside Wharf, crossing Dumers Lane on the level, and proceeding northwards and under Bury Road. Contemporary maps indicate the line as 'tramway', suggesting, perhaps, that the gauge was not standard but narrow. After the 1914-1918 War, the track remained in situ, eventually to be covered by other land uses, its purpose no longer of value.

The first Radcliffe Bridge station opened for public use on 25th September 1846 by the ELR, with subsequent rebuilding and alterations carried out by the LYR. Up to 1874, this was Radcliffe's main station, an intermediate stopping place between Manchester and Bury as far as ELR/LYR operations were concerned, but a vital point of arrival and departure for travellers to and from the town.

An event which reached the local press occurred in November 1877 when the town was bathed in a pea-soup fog, the bane of all railway operators. This involved an express train running between Scotland and the Midlands, due to arrive at Manchester Victoria at 9.50 pm. Instead, it crashed into a goods engine going about its business in the murk at Radcliffe Bridge Station, "with serious consequences."

"A few yards on the Manchester side of the station, a goods engine, which had been employed in shunting, was standing upon the Up line, and with it the express train came into collision." *Middleton Albion* November 17th 1877

It appeared at the time that it was driver error; he had not seen a distant signal which had warned of a home signal set at danger. Despite shutting off steam and the application of Fay's Patent brake applied to the rear five carriages, the collision took place at 9.55 p.m., shaking the ground in the close vicinity. Fog signals had not been used and as luck would have it, the express had slowed from a speed of 40 mph to 5 mph. Despite damage to both engines and the smashing of the first two carriages, there were no fatalities; instead was a pile of debris which was cleared the following day by lunchtime.

The LYR's line between Manchester Victoria and Bury via Whitefield and Prestwich originated in the New Line Act of July 18th 1872 which included a new station, known as Radcliffe New Station and a link from a junction, just south of the station, bearing north west to Bradley Fold Junction [the Bradley Fold Extension]. One advantage of this link was the provision of an alternative route between Manchester and Bolton, (although two miles longer than the direct route via Farnworth), the contract being given to T.J. Waller for the work undertaken between Cheetham Hill and Radcliffe, and the link to Bradley Fold (Waller's tender was £293,500).

A later LYR Act of June 21st 1877 authorised the provision of a west-north fork (West Fork: 52 chains) between West Junction and North Junction, the contract again given to Waller who had been so success-

Radcliffe South Junction at rail level, circa 1916. The station is in its most complete form with a ridge and furrow canopy over each platform. At the southern end of the station stands Radcliffe South Junction signal box: as LYR box 362, it opened in 1898, its 33 lever frame facing the Manchester - Bolton line. Notice the alternation of the third-rail from one side of the running line to the other, and the 'ramp' at the extreme end to enable the collector shoes to glide easily into position on contact. To the left is a siding with third-rail used by trains laying over between peak hour services. *National Railway Museum (Horwich F1654).*

ful on the Cheetham Hill-Bradley Fold section.

The Board of Trade sanctioned the use of these lines in September 1879 and a Manchester Victoria to Bury steam-hauled service began in the September of that year. The Radcliffe Junction to Bradley Fold link and the West Fork were also opened to traffic by December 1st 1879. Thus, in the years before electric trains were to pass through Radcliffe, steam-hauled trains served the town: Manchester to Bury; Manchester to Bolton via Bradley Fold, and unusually Bolton to Bacup via Bury Bolton Street.

Services on the electrified Manchester to Bury main line were established in February 1916, representing what was generally understood at the time to be an initial stage in the electrification of several routes north of Manchester. One consequence of the electrification scheme was the abandonment of steam-hauled trains running between Manchester and Bolton via Radcliffe. Instead, steam-hauled trains started at Radcliffe and ran the route via Bradley Fold Junction and Darcy Lever to Bolton Trinity Street. From the start of 1918, these steam services were placed in the hands of LYR rail-motors, similar to those which had plied the Holcombe Brook branch [LMS Nos.10600 and 10617 operated this service and were known variously as "Puffing Billy" and "Bowton Billy"].

> "It had a very short boiler and pushed and pulled the carriage, dependent on whether it was coming or going (at Radcliffe) if an extra carriage was put on in the rush hour, the engine was often between them, pushing one and pulling the other." *Was My Journey Really Necessary?* F.Campbell.

A small lineside station was erected at Ainsworth Road about 1 mile from Radcliffe, this coming into service on January 1st 1918. Very basic in layout and facilities, the halt had no platforms, the railmotors

having retractable steps to facilitate the movement of passengers on and off the trains. In the later 1940s The Halt was redesigned to conform with normal platform arrangements in preparation for the abandonment of rail-motors in 1947. Prior to this, it was necessary for a set of wooden steps to be used.

Part of the electrification scheme at Radcliffe included the construction of a sub-station which received high voltage from the LYR power station at Clifton and then converted the current to 1200 volts dc. Tenders were invited by the LYR in June 1914 for the "erection of an Electric Sub-station and Battery House at Radcliffe". The sub-station was a large brick building sited on a piece of land between the Manchester, Bolton & Bury Canal and the West Fork. Power to the sub-station was conveyed by overhead conductors carried on H-poles over a distance of 4 miles. The building originally housed 3 rotary convertors (ac-dc) and three transformers (step-down 6600v - 1200v) plus 580 battery cells for use as an auxiliary backup in the event of a mains failure. (There was just enough capacity to move a train a short distance to a siding or station in the event of a power breakdown). On closure of the Clifton Power Station in 1933, current was then taken from the CEGBs National Grid supply which had been set up in 1926. In LMS days and later, the substation was always manned by two operatives working on a shift system, every day of the year, with the exception of night, when the system was shut down. Large electrical lever switches enabled sections of track to be isolated between section gaps when maintenance or emergency required a 'dead' track. The building could only be reached on foot from the canal towpath, a footpath bordering the Cricket Ground (via a locked gate) or by alighting a train standing on the West Fork.

(left) **Radcliffe in the summer of 1935. This aerial view well illustrates the railway infrastructure in the town during those LMS days of the mid-1930's. Firstly the general layout: the long curving line from top left (from Whitefield) to bottom left (to Bury) is the 'lecky' line. At centre top, the viaduct of the Irwell appears to be casting a shadow towards Wilton Mill. At South Junction, the Bolton line heads off to the right; just visible on the right, middle, is the bridge carrying the Bolton line over the straight Clifton Jct to Bury line (extreme right to bottom left). Radcliffe West fork can be seen curving across the bottom portion of the photograph (North Junction to West Junction, left to right). Radcliffe Central station, minus canopy over platform 1, is neatly situated in the V of South Junction, platform 3's canopy is intact. Note the wide Railway Approach and the landscaped shallow banking either side, studded with bushes. Also the expanse of bare ground (now Festival Gardens)which lies to the east of the 'Sandhills' east of the 'lecky' line. The goods depot is well-stocked with lines of wagons consisting of open wagons (probably loaded with coal and esparto grass), and several vans. The levelled ground, occupied by the yard, is at a lower level than the electric lines and the Bolton line. The extensions to the goods sheds can be clearly seen in the altered roof styles. The roof of the electricity sub-station appears at the foot of the photograph. The H-poles bringing power from Outwood Power Station cast short shadows, suggesting that the photograph was taken between mid day and mid-afternoon. Other dominant features include Wilton Mill, with its smoking chimney, Spring Lane Brewery, close to the electric line, the footpath from Spring to Coney Green, the allotment gardens and, of course, the seemingly endless rows of terraced houses which characterized many northern industrial towns.** *Aerofilms courtesy Bury Library.*

The western side of Radcliffe goods yard in the 1950s, a view as seen from the footpath to Coney Green which bridged the Clifton Jct to Bury line at this location. Beyond the lines of mineral wagons and vans is the extension to the goods shed, the bush on the right marking the approximate position of the old goods shed which stood aside the Up line to Clifton Jct. *Radcliffe Library.*

This photograph was taken in January 1954 from the junction of Bury Road and Spring Lane and looked towards the rear of platform 4. This was half-hidden by a steep bank, the remains of Sandhills, the sandy overburden excavated from Whitefield Cutting and dumped here by the contractor. *Authors collection.*

Radcliffe Goods Yard - It is thought that a goods yard of sorts existed at Radcliffe Bridge station as soon as the ELR decided on the conveyance of goods in 1847. The *Manchester Guardian* carried a contract advert on 12th February 1848 which stated:

"The East Lancashire Railway announces tenders for the erection of station buildings and goods warehouses on the railway. Some of the buildings will be entirely of timber."

This then was the first Radcliffe goods facilities, but the 1850s map shows no development on the ground which became the site of Radcliffe Goods Yard. It was then open land on the northern side of Spring Lane, occupied by a single homestead, Ousel Fold. By 1878, the goods yard which had developed on this land consisted of seven curved sidings, each leading off a lay-by siding on the Up-side. A cross-over linked one of the sidings to the Down-side at the Withins Lane end, whilst adjacent to Spring Lane, there were three buildings, one of which was a warehouse into which one siding entered at the northern end.

The 1907 map reveals that the capacity of the yard had increased in response to the growth of industry in Radcliffe. There were now 17 dead-end sidings, two of which penetrated a new long goods shed, the original 1878 shed still standing and served by a single siding. A smaller goods shed had been added at some stage alongside the Up-line and near the bridge which carried the footpath over the ELR line. The yard also had offices along Spring Lane, directly opposite Railway Approach which gave access to Radcliffe New Station. Three yard cranes served the yard.

Six years later, the yard showed little change. However, the 1907 goods shed had been extended southwards by about 100 feet, following the curvature of the sidings which passed through it. Appearing in *The Railway News*, August 3, 1912, D.C.Rattray, Chief Civil Engineer for the LYR, reported;

"On the extension of the grain and cotton warehouse, offices etc, at Radcliffe; the shed for paper traffic is completed and brought into use. The foundations for the extension of the grain and cotton warehouse are finished, and the whole of the works comprised in the contract are about two-thirds finished."

By 1929, six years into LMS ownership, one additional siding gave the total sidings as 18. The old goods shed of 1878 had been extended northwards from an original length of 100 feet to 200 feet. Two weigh machines had been added to the yard with a reduction of yard cranes to two. In 1937, the yard remained the same with 18 dead-end sidings. The two largest warehouses were still functioning, but the smallest shed next to the Up-line had been removed. Yard cranes and weigh machines were still intact with offices for weighing coal, and stables backed on to Spring Lane. The yard cranes were at the end of their lives even in the 1920s, one described by Fred Campbell as 'a real antique':

"It had a massive gear wheel which was operated by a huge crank handle turned by two men. It was used for round timber, forgings, iron bars and such things the lifting of which was a slow and laborious procedure". *Was My Journey Really Necessary?*

To railwaymen working in the yard, the 18 sidings were known by name and number. New recruits had to learn the sequence of tracks as they came off the main line, and their relative position in the yard. It all served the purpose of efficiency and enhanced smooth operations. At Radcliffe, the first six sidings followed the number scheme, 1-6, but from number 7, the sidings carried an appellation according to some long-held use, some obvious, others unclear as to the meaning of their name. No.7 was referred to as "One Field", No.8, "Two Field", No.9 "Back Road", No.10 "Warehouse Road", No.11 "New Siding", No.12 "Old Siding" and No.13 "Crane Road". Nos.14-18 had names, now lost in the mists of time.

Occasionally, even the generous siding capacity was outstripped by the number of wagons in need of stabling. The excess wagons were 'stood out' in sidings just outside the town, at Hagside Siding, Canal Siding and Withins Siding. Whether in the yard or 'standing out', a careful check had to be made on the wagon number, its position, disposition, (loaded or empty) and the kind of load carried. It was not uncommon for 100 wagons to be 'standing out' whilst awaiting accommodation in the yard.

The volume of goods traffic at Radcliffe in LMS days (and into British Railways days) was very large relative to the size of the town. Much of the freight was in the form of raw materials for local industries: the paper industry alone required large amounts of wood pulp and Esparto grass which arrived in Radcliffe from Preston Docks and the Manchester Docks periodically. The East Lancashire Paper Mill had its own battery-driven collection and delivery vehicles which carried finished paper to the yard and when necessary, returned with bales of Esparto grass. Some of the bales would burst, liberating the yellow grass to drift about the yard like tumbleweed after a delivery from the docks. To handle the goods traffic, Radcliffe yard had a complement of men and boys whose needs were met by the provision of mess huts and shunter's cabins, not far from the entrance on Spring Lane. In winter, and at night, the mess huts were a haven or refuge from the wet and cold. Fred Campbell described the mess rooms as 'focal points', not only for railway staff but also got "anybody who had occasion to visit the depot. There was always a blazing fire, a hot oven for warming dinners, and facilities for brewing."

The yard also possessed stables in which a number of shire horses were kept. It was a common sight in the 1920s and 1930s for horses to plod through the town delivering goods to various manufacturing concerns. Near the yard, in the triangle of land south of West Fork, lay open land partly occupied by a somewhat bumpy cricket ground. It was on to this grassy area that the horses were put to graze during the Wakes holidays, earning an annual week's rest from their labours.

Routes Through Radcliffe - *Radcliffe Central to Bradley Fold Junction -* The approach to Radcliffe Central Station from Whitefield, carried the railway through the deep and wide Whitefield Cutting on a falling gradient beneath Radcliffe New Road and alongside Coronation Park. The cutting gave way on the approach to Radcliffe Viaduct, (Bridge No.43), 230 yards long, 12 arches of 40 feet span, a stone edifice which carried the line over Milltown Street and the Irwell. Unlike most of the railway infrastructure in the town, the viaduct still exists, carrying the Metro line to Bury from Manchester. It is worthy of inspection today. Two of its arches span the river and unlike the other ten, are skewed, both piers rising from the river bed. Once across the viaduct, the line

Railway Approach leading to the main entrance of Radcliffe Central station in January 1954. Platform 2 was on the right and platform 3 the left. The rear of platform 3 was at one time the same as platform 2 giving the impression of a mirror image from this viewpoint. *Authors collection.*

Radcliffe West Junction, 7th March 1962. The lines to the right of the signal box ran straight as a die into Central station while the lines branching off to the left (Radcliffe West Fork) curved round to join the 'lecky' line at Radcliffe North Junction. The building on the left is Radcliffe substation. Radcliffe West Junction signal box opened in 1920, housed a LYR 28 lever frame; it closed in November 1964. Absent in this scene are the former Canal sidings which ran behind the signal box, and Whittaker Bridge Sidings which occupied the land where the row of telegraph poles are. *F. Collinge.*

reached South Junction which marked the point where the Bolton and Bury lines diverged, both routes crossing Church Street West on an arched bridge before entering Central Station. South Junction signalbox (LYR wooden 1898) stood on the platform between the two routes, an important location for a box at the southern end of the station.

The line to Bolton ran through the west side of the station, which could be approached by various means; the main vehicular entrance was on 'Railway Approach', running off Spring Lane; a sloping footpath from Church Street West leading pedestrians diagonally up the west-facing embankment and an early rear entrance beneath Church Street West bridge, the 12 feet wide blocked-up arch clearly visible from the street level.

Radcliffe Central (known as Radcliffe New Station between 1879 and the summer of 1933) had four platforms, number 4 being the Bury-Manchester platform on the electric line. The 1937 O.S. plan shows that all four platforms had canopies (of the ridge and furrow type) extending northwards from the main building, but an aerial photograph dated 1935 indicates that platform 4 had lost its canopy (there were certainly four canopies in 1916). The loss of the canopy by 1935 heralded the gradual demise of the platform for everyday use; by 1950, it was used only for excursion trains, the push-pull Radcliffe to Bolton service operating from platform 2.

The main booking office stood on the ground floor at the top of Railway Approach - the bowels of the station had to be entered before the booking office was reached. Stairs connected the ground floor to each platform and a lift enabled parcels to be transferred from one level to another. Other space in the booking hall area were taken by stores, porters' room, general and ladies waiting rooms, WCs and station master's office. At platform level, it was number 4 which boasted the main passenger facilities, comprising a general waiting room, ladies waiting room and toilets.

On either side of the entrance to Railway Approach, were buildings serving coal merchants and the general public: four wooden huts stood on Spring Lane and were used as coal merchants' offices, whilst the passing public made use of a sweet shop just inside the approach.

Up to the 1960s, it was common for newspapers to be carried by the railway to stations along routes leading out of Manchester. At the appropriate time, usually between 4 p.m. and 5 p.m., the Approach would be thronged with newspaper boys awaiting the arrival of the *Manchester Evening News*, adding to the daily hustle and bustle of this junction station.

Both routes through the station were double track and uncomplicated. To the south of the station on the Down side Bolton line, an electrified kick-back siding with a trap-point trailed back just before Church Street west bridge. The line left the station on an embankment in a north westerly direction, firstly over Spring Lane and then over the Clifton Jct to Bury line on a girder bridge, passed Railway Wagon Works on the left and the extensive goods sidings on the right. From here the line passed into what was then open country: to the right West Fork could be seen curving in on a shallow embankment, the intervening flat ground occupied partly by a cricket ground. The line crossed an occupation bridge over a footpath to Whittaker Street (where the old fire station and public baths were located) and then over the Manchester, Bolton & Bury Canal at the so-called Whittaker's Bridge. The 1850s map shows Whittaker's Bridge as an occupation bridge carrying a farm track from Springs Lane via Whittaker's Farm and beyond to Coney Green Farm. during the passage of time and coupled with many alterations undertaken in this area, the name seems to have been transferred to the

This impressive network of lines occurred at Radcliffe North Junction, and here devoid of running trains on 22nd April 1962. The building on the left is Withins Mill and next to it Withins Siding on which a rake of 21 ton loco coal wagons have been stabled, awaiting movement to Bury shed. The tall signal box on the Up side of the main line is Radcliffe North Junction box, the structure built to improve sighting over Withins Mill roof. The three lines curving to the left head for Radcliffe Central; the straight-ahead lines ran to Radcliffe Bridge station, whilst the pair of lines curving to the right form the West Fork to Bradley Fold Junction. To the right is a short overlap spur at the southern end of Hagside Siding. *F. Collinge.*

railway bridge. The Bolton line continued on a straight course to meet the West Fork at West Junction, the triangle of land between the two routes and the canal occupied by the farm track to Coney Green, and a looped siding (Canal Siding) which trailed back from the Fork to terminate near the canal bank at a wagon turntable and a short spur leading off at 90 degrees. Here, there was a coal chute and a 22 ton crane for heavy lifting jobs.

West Junction signal box (LYR brick 1920) stood in the V of the two lines, occupying a pleasant, semi-rural location. Beyond the junction the line ran under Belgrave Street bridge and then beneath a footbridge, the outlook on both sides over allotment gardens, the line continuing on an upward gradient of 1 in 88. Once under Cemetery Road bridge (the site of Coney Green Colliery nearby), the route curved to the west in a long cutting, heading for Black Lane, a district of Radcliffe. One mile 10 chains from Radcliffe Central, to the west of Ainsworth Road bridge, the LYR had erected a small halt in 1918 to serve the Black Lane commuters to Bolton and Manchester. The halt consisted in LMS days of two concrete platforms, the Up side having a single modest

shelter, both sides of the halt accessible by diagonally sloping footpaths from Ainsworth Road. the station must have been uninspiring to the photographic brethren during those days before closure in 1953, since no photographs have been obtained to illustrate the location.

Beyond Ainsworth Road Halt, the line continued to curve to the west in a diminishing cutting, out once again into open pastures, crossed by an occupation footbridge, and then met by a long siding on the Up side which trailed back from Bradley Fold Junction.

Ringley Road station to Buckley Wells.

Ringley Road station had been opened by the East Lancashire Railway on 31st May 1847. It was set in a semi-rural area lying south west of Radcliffe and was the second station after leaving Clifton Junction some 2 miles 30 chains further on. Harrison and Sale, in their 1849 guide, make no mention of it, concentrating instead on describing the landscape as it appeared from the window of train chugging on towards Ringley Road.

"Skirting the east side of the Valley of the Irwell a fine view is gained of the vale, with its shady dells, green knolls and clumps of trees dotted here and there with white houses and tall chimneys."

The station was located adjacent to Ringley Road and Wood Street in Radcliffe's district of Outwood. Two lengthy platforms comprised the modest

Ringley Road station circa 1920. This is a poor photograph but has been included to illustrate the station in the absence of better which are decidedly rare. Worthy of mention is the cinder/gravel platform surface, the lower quadrant signal mounted on a wooden post, and the Ringley road bridge which is supported by timber trusses presumably while repairs to the bridge are carried out. In this area of mining, subsidence was a constant menace which affected bridges, buildings, roads and permanent way. *Tom Wray coll.*

facility, sited in a deep long cutting, overlooked on the east by Outwood Colliery brickworks in LYR and LMS days, and little else save two rows of terraced houses - "Yew Tree Houses". A long footpath connected the Down platform with Ringley Road and the top end of Wood Street, whilst the Up side could be gained by use of a subway at the southern end of the station. The only station building stood on the Down platform, amounting to no more than a ticket office and waiting room housed under a slated hipped roof which overhung the platform to provide a narrow awning. One wonders why a station existed there at all in such a sparsely populated area, but its function was to serve the Outwood area generally which contained a scatter of residential properties and much industry.

The line between Ringley Road and Radcliffe Bridge station passed through land long ravaged by mining and other industry, on a falling gradient of 1 in 120. The old ELR line bore north eastwards under an occupation bridge and entered a complex of sidings, namely, Outwood Sidings on the west side, and Outwood Colliery Sidings on the east. The latter were associated with the largest coal mine in the Radcliffe area, Outwood Colliery, which, in its heyday, had employed 2,000 men, a "focal point of industry in the town and the hub of the community". The first ELR trains slowly wending their way northwards would have past coal mining activities in the 1840s: a small mine known as 'Cloughside' had existed before its expansion into Outwood Colliery, its coal having previously being transported by a tramway to the Manchester, Bolton & Bury Canal at Ringley Wharf. In 1931, Outwood Colliery was closed due to an underground fire which caused the collapse of the winding gear into its own shaft. By the middle 1930s, only the remains of the mine were extant, leaving extensive sidings as reminders of what used to be.

Outwood Sidings formed a series of looped roads which allowed the movement and stabling of coal wagons serving the Lancashire Electric Power Company's generating station at Outward, Radcliffe. The original power station had been opened by Lord Derby on October 1905 and was the first power station to transmit 10,000v to its customers by bare overhead conductors. The coal supply from Outwood Sidings was brought to a single siding elevated at 70 feet above the base of the building.

> "The trucks were hauled by an electric locomotive crane, which was also used for tipping. At the end of and under the sidings, there was a containing hopper into which the coal was emptied." *Electricity in Manchester* - R.Frost.

Short spurs of rail track ran at 90 degrees to the elevated siding and into the generation plant so that coal could be fed into the boiler-house bunkers. The electric locomotive referred to, obtained its power from an overhead catenary system which spanned the sidings and elevated line, terminating before the junction with the main Down running line. On the Up side, Outwood Colliery Sidings led back to form a stub of six sidings and a long looped siding which extended as far as the colliery brick works near Ringley Road. Near the Colliery Sidings were Radcliffe Corporation Sewage Works facing, across the railway, Outwood Siding signal box (LYR brick 1874).

Beyond the siding complex, the main line was crossed by an L-shaped footbridge which carried a footpath from Freightman Hillock Farm to the power station. At this point, a further array of sidings spread out north eastwards, comprising 'Washery Sidings', on both sides of a large reservoir. The main area of Washery Sidings passed to the south of the reservoir and into yet another siding complex known as 'James Street Sidings'. The Washery Sidings and James Street Sidings combined to give ample accommodation for hundreds of coal wagons from different collieries in the area, the Washery continuing to separate slack from coal, and wash the latter until its closure in 1956.

The railway between Ringley Road and the Irwell, thus passed through colliery wasteland of sludge beds, slack heaps and general dereliction which is normally associated with the extraction of coal. On the ap-

proach to the famous Irwell the line crossed a colliery tramway which was probably used to carry slack waste to a tip on the west side of the railway. The approach to the viaduct was on an embankment overlooking the Irwell Bleach & Dyeworks on the left. It was at this location in January 1899 that a major landslip occurred on a Saturday morning affecting forty yards of embankment which slumped downslope, leaving the rails suspended in mid-air. The *Manchester Guardian* reported the matter in its Monday 2nd January issue:

> "Tons of soil slipped into the lodge of water below to a neighbouring dyeworks, causing the water to overflow the bank, and for some time it was thought the bank might give way. the works had to be closed owing to the muddy condition of the water!"

This day time occurrence was quickly reported to Manchester and Bury and the traffic on the line was diverted via the Prestwich line and Bolton, single line working being established later in the day.

The original ELR viaduct was of timber construction built by contractors for the company in 1846. In 1881, this was replaced by the LYR, the contractor Andrew Handyside, carrying out the work for £4,225. In 1923 the LMS carried out deck repairs and the viaduct became No.12. Remains of the viaduct can be inspected today and is well worth a visit, although access on to the structure is prohibited and a steel fence prevents access at both ends. However, a good view may be obtained and will reveal the bare bones of the 1881 rebuild. Five arched cast iron girders of 55 feet span are mounted on four brick piers, two of which are supported on masonry embedded in the river bed. Each arch is made up of six ribs transversely connected by iron joiners which support a wooden decking. The arches still bear a numeral, number 5 being at the northern end. For safety purposes the viaduct carried a line of iron railings on each side, these now gradually disintegrating along with the masonry at the viaduct ends. 340 feet long, the viaduct is 70 feet above the river and carried the line on to another embankment leading to Sion Street underbridge.

Radcliffe Bridge station, (more commonly known as Radcliffe Old Station) was located between Sion Street and Green Street, ranking as the town's second station after the opening of New Station in 1879. In LYR and LMS days, it consisted of two platforms, the Up side accessible from Railway Street and Green Street, the Down side from Green Street, a lattice footbridge connecting both platforms. The main station building stood on the Up platform, stone-built with a hipped slate roof and narrow wooden awning which projected from the length of the building. The Down side possessed a wooden shelter with a hipped slate roof, without awning. Also on this side of the line was a small goods shed, its east wall lined against the platform, the small yard served by a short dead-end siding which continued under the footbridge from a trailing point on the Down line. Radcliffe Bridge goods yard for many years held the merit of being the main embarkation stage for cattle which were driven into the town on the hoof to the local abattoir. At the southern end of the Down platform ramp stood Radcliffe Bridge station signal box (LYR wood 1909).

From beyond Green Street, the line ran in a cutting on a gentle curve to the north east, passed Blackburn Street underbridge and on towards Spring Lane Bridge and the bridge bearing the Radcliffe to Bolton line. The route from Radcliffe Bridge station to this point had cut through back streets on the northern outskirts of the town, but now reached a more open vista albeit dominated at first by Radcliffe Goods Yard on the right. A metal girder bridge carried the footpath from Spring Lane to Coney Green Farm (during the construction of the 1878/9 Radcliffe New Station to Bradley Fold line, there was much alteration to existing footpaths near the railway) and from here the line ran alongside the north western edge of the goods yard towards Radcliffe North Junction where it was joined by both East and West Forks.

The junction was controlled by Radcliffe North Jct Signal box (LYR brick 1879) which was sited on the Up side of the main line. Beyond

Radcliffe Central 26.1.1954. This was the busy side of the station. The view is from the Down Manchester - Bury (platform 3) towards platform 4 from which trains from Bury to Manchester would halt. Again, there is extensive use of timber, relieved by the protruding ornate brick stacks. In the murky distance, left, stood Wilton Mill, only recently demolished. *Authors collection.*

this, the line was accompanied briefly by an elbow of the Manchester. Bolton & Bury Canal to the left, whilst on the Up side, Withins Mill, itself served a single siding, marked the location of Hagside Siding which ran parallel to the Down main line for some 430 yards, entered from a crossover connection opposite Withins Mill. The line here was crossed by iron hogsback bridge carrying a lane from Bury Road to Yew Trees Farm. It was at this point that the ephemeral Withins Station was erected by the ELR to serve Radcliffe (not Radcliffe Bridge) meeting an early demise in 1851.

From here, the line curved northwards through a rural landscape between the old canal and Bury Road. At Lower Hagside, Eton Hill Road (now Warth Fold Road) ran alongside the Up line as far as Bank Top, a cluster of terraced houses on either side of the line. Here, Bealey's Goyt, an artificial water channel commenced conveying water to Bealey's Dyeworks in Dumer's Lane Radcliffe, the line crossing the great river on a ELR iron lattice girder bridge (No.22) of 100 feet 7 inch. span. This bridge is unusual in that it was (and still is) a span of iron about 4-6 feet above the river, with a combined walkway below rail level, which permitted pedestrians to cross the river. The walkway was made up of wooden planks laid transversely to the bridge, access gained to it by way of an arched subway built into the stonework at either end. The subway at the southern end still takes a footpath from Bank Top to Hinds Lane. The bridge is locally known as 'Monkey Bridge', owing to the cage-like structure of its lattice work.

Bank Top is an interesting place, not only because of Monkey Bridge but by dint of the level crossing and Hagside signal box which once stood on the Up side with its back facing Eton Hill Road, an LYR brick box of 1873 vintage. Originally a mining community, Bank Top benefitted from the canal which could be used to carry coal from the seven pits in the area.

"Bank Top must have had a fair population, for when the East Lancashire Railway arrived in 1846, it was favoured with a station named Radcliffe North. For some reason, however, it appears to have been little used and after four years it was closed". *An Intimate Look at Bury's Old Canal* F.Campbell.

Once across the bridge, the view to the right was dominated by Warth

Mills, a brick mill occupying land close to the river. The mill has been all but reduced to its foundations and is now the home of Macpherson Paints and Kembia Powders in superimposed modern buildings.

The line continued towards Buckley Wells on an embankment, over an occupation bridge near a Methodist Church at Warth Fold hamlet, curving north west on its approach to Bury. The occupation bridge is an archway in stone, the lane passing under the railway once allowing access into a large field upon which cattle were grazed following their journey on the hoof via Openshaw Fold Road from Knowsley Street cattle pens.

To the left, a bend in the river neared the railway and then diverged from it again, whilst to the right, Openshaw Fold Road neared the railway, ran alongside and then bore away towards Manchester Old Road. At Bury Loco Junction, the Bury Loop joined the main line and was the location for Bury Loco Junction signal box, sited on the Up side (LYR wood 1898). From here, the main line entered Buckley Wells marked by an increase in trackwork, locomotive shed, electric car shed, Buckley Wells crossing and Coal Sidings. Within a distance of 20 chains, Bolton Street station was reached, 10 miles from Manchester.

(above) **Radcliffe Central 26.1.1954.** The view, taken from the Radcliffe - Bolton platform (No.1) looking east towards Radcliffe South Jct signal box. Of interest is the extensive use of timber for the buildings and the prosaic method of supporting the unglazed platform canopy. Note also that the 3rd rail extended from the junction with the line to Bury and continued as far as the end of the station. During L&Y, LMS and early BR days, there were peak hour electric workings between Radcliffe and Manchester Victoria using platforms 1 and 2. *Authors collection.*

(right) **Radcliffe Central 26.1.1954.** Whilst awaiting the electric train to Manchester, this was the scene which confronted you - platform 3, the Down line to Bury. The canopy over platform 3 appears to have been cut back at some stage: pre-war plans show the canopy to have extended further although it was shorter than the one facing. *Authors collection.*

(right) **Radcliffe Central 1954.** A view of the southern end of the station this time from the little-used platform 1 and looking towards the Bolton - Manchester platform 2. The somewhat dwarf brick wall on platform 2 supported the roof over the booking office, stores and parcels office on the ground floor. Notice the absence of the original LYR valence along the canopy front. *Authors collection*

(opposite) **The station interior in January 1954.** The timber columns and trusses are shown to good effect on the landing which connected platforms 2 and 3. The view is towards platform 3, the 'way out' sign indicating a flight of stairs which led down to the lower level and exit via Railway Approach. The brick wall, doors and windows, formed the inner wall of the trapezium-shaped structure which can be seen in previous photograph. Note the tiled non-slip floor, customary baggage trolley and mandatory firebuckets hanging from wall brackets. *Authors collection.*

(left) A rear view of a Bury-bound two-car e.m.u. crossing the Irwell Viaduct as it nears Radcliffe Central on 29th April 1971. From this vantage point close to Coronation Park, it is possible to see not only the fully functioning platforms 3 and 4, but also the remains of platform 1 curving off to the left. In the distance, in line with the station, it is just possible to make out Radcliffe sub-station. *Radcliffe Library.*

(opposite top) A close-up view of platform 2 in July 1959, looking towards Whitefield. The boast that Radcliffe "has the most modern railway station in Lancashire" can be substantiated by this photograph which shows the 1960s no-nonsense, straight-forward functionalism which prevailed - a far cry from the creaking, soot-stained aromatic LYR facilities which had character if nothing else. Pieces of the original infrastructure remain: Radcliffe South Junction signal box; the platform parcel trolley; the bull-head rails and the semaphore signalling. *Radcliffe Library.*

(opposite bottom) A further view north on the same day. Apart from the expanse of fresh chippings, the platforms have been surfaced with asphalt and edged with concrete slabs. Note that platform 3 is bereft of passenger accommodation and is now served by a single line, the Down line having been truncated beyond the station. *Radcliffe Library.*

(below) A view from the junction of Rectory Lane and Church Street West, in January 1954, the latter passing under the bridge towards Radcliffe town centre. Once again the steep bank up to platform 4 is evident, most of Sandhills was removed by the Council to convert the area into Festival Gardens in 1951. *Authors collection.*

112

"....the most modern railway station in Lancashire...."

The Radcliffe Times of 5th June 1959 reported the official inspection of the town's modern station and was justifiably proud of the 'new' amenity, following two years of campaigning for the improvement for an "improved and brighter station for Radcliffe."

"Sir Brian Robertson, Chairman of the British Transport Commission, inspected the new £110,000 rebuilt Central station and went aboard one of the new trains which was drawn up at the station for his visit... Sir Brian, who arrived with the other railway officials in a personal diesel fitted with armchairs and travelling sitting room, was conducted round the station by Station Master W. Brook... There were still some workmen busy on touching-up jobs on the station when he arrived, but the army of workmen who had been clambering over the station at the weekend in the last minute rush, were absent. Sir Brian, a former general, gave the building a military-type inspection. He strode purposefully into every room of the building, including the ladies toilet....."

Contrasting fortunes: *(top)* **Radcliffe Central 27.7.59. A view of the renumbered platforms (numbers 4 and 3 becoming 1 and 2 respectively), looking towards Bury. Absent are the original brick platform faces, the timber ridge and furrow canopies and the trapezium-shaped platform level building which covered the booking hall, store rooms and parcel office. The 1960's look comprises the use of pre-cast concrete panelling; glazed steel framed waiting rooms; new brick station building and steel-framed and sheeted integral canopies; modern electric lamp standards fluorescent lighting and the expanded metal fencing.** *Radcliffe Library.*

(bottom) **Radcliffe Bridge station sometime after closure which occurred on 5th July 1958. Having the distinction of being the town's first station, opened by the ELR in 1846, the amenity looks worn out and neglected. Weeds (the ubiquitous Rose Bay Willow herb) are beginning to colonise the crumbling platforms. Note the arched windows and the stout stone sills in the building, betraying its ELR origin, and the sagging platform canopy, supported by two steel uprights bedded into the platform.** *Radcliffe Library.*

A monument to Victorian engineering prowess, Andrew Handyside's rebuilt viaduct which carried the Clifton Junction to Bury line over the Irwell. We can only imagine the sense of awe and trepidation felt by the pioneering group of passengers on that inaugural day of 25th September 1846, as they were drawn slowly across the then recently completed viaduct, which in those days had timber spans. Here we see the forlorn disposition of the structure in more modern times. The timber decking (replaced by the LMS in 1923) and the tubular parapet rails show signs of rot and rust, rendering the viaduct decidedly unsafe. For safety reasons, both ends are sealed off to prevent access, deliberate or accidental. A more modern expedient has been to take advantage of the pier arches to accommodate a pipeline. Outwood viaduct, as it is known, is a Grade 2 listed structure. *Radcliffe Library*.

(above) **Outwood Colliery Sidings and Outwood Sidings signal box, 8th April 1962.** To the left is Outwood (Radcliffe) Power Station, with its distinctive roof-top, cylindrical chimneys. A line of wagons occupy Lord Derby's Siding "under the wires", the latter an electrification in miniature for use by an electric shunter/crane. Note the sleeper fence which bordered this section of the railway-owned land. Ownership of land was important as shown by a comment in the 'General Appendix to the Working Time Table' of January 1931: "At the Ringley Road and Radcliffe ends of the Outwood colliery Sidings, six notice boards, indicating the limits beyond which Railway Company's engines must not pass, are provided, and the instructions thereon must be strictly observed by all concerned". *F Collinge.*

(left) **A close-up of Outwood Sidings and signal box, 8th April 1962.** Opened in 1874, the box was possibly partially rebuilt in 1895 acquiring a new timber top in that year. It housed an LYR 28 lever frame and stood with its rear wall facing Lord Derby's Siding and the electrified power station sidings. The whole place at this time had an air of dereliction and untidiness even though it was a working siding. The post-war boom was with us "..we had never had it so good...", but lack of investment in industry and undisciplined practices around the work places ensured that the good times would not last and others would take our place as the "Workshop of the world". *F.Collinge.*

(left) **The front elevation of Outwood Sidings signal box in June 1957.** Set in a area of industrially despoiled land adjacent to the power station, the box opened as LYR 317 on the Down side between Ringley Road station and Radcliffe Bridge station, closing on the 29th December 1964. *Tom Wray.*

Chapter 7. THE MANCHESTER - BURY ELECTRICS

LYR Pioneering Prowess - dc unorthodoxy.

"Gradual additions to the electric sections in the Liverpool area have rendered the Lancashire and Yorkshire system a relatively comprehensive one, and in due course extensions into other districts were to be anticipated. We understand that the Directors have decided to electrify the railway from Manchester via Prestwich and Radcliffe to Bury. The trains will be worked with direct current collected from a third rail, as on the Southport line".
Railway News 3rd January 1914.

In true pioneering spirit, the LYR had developed an 18 mile electrified route by March 1904, running between Liverpool Exchange and Southport (Crossens). This was a third-rail 630 volts dc system, promoted by Aspinall the LYR's General Manager and mentor, along with electrical equipment and expertise developed by Dick, Kerr & Co.Ltd, a firm which was to figure largely in future developments around Bury. Following successful experimentation with electrification on the Holcombe Brook Branch in 1912/13, the LYR, once again under Aspinall's guidance turned its attention to a broader scheme of electrification in the north Manchester area, including routes to Oldham, Rochdale and Bury and Bolton. However, only Bury was to be granted an electrified route from Manchester, the drive for such schemes coinciding with the outbreak of the Great War in 1914.

The route for a Manchester to Bury electrified line was already in existence by the turn of the century. The New Lines Act of 18th July 1872 had established a link between Manchester Victoria and Radcliffe by way of the expanding districts of Cheetham, Crumpsall, Heaton Park, Prestwich and Whitefield, the new line forming a junction with the inveterate ELR line at Radcliffe North Junction. The contract for this work was let to Thomas James Walker for £293,000 on 23rd February 1876 and included the link between Radcliffe South Junction and Bradley Fold Junction.

John Marshall refers to the "formidable difficulties" involved in the construction of the mile long Whitefield Cutting, this problem alone raising the expenditure on the scheme by £55,000 in April 1878.

The potential for passenger traffic was considerable. The populations of the above-named districts were expanding rapidly at the turn of the century. Taking Prestwich as an example, the population had risen from 12,766 in 1901 to 17,915 in 1911, most of this growth stemming from

outward migration of population from Manchester's older suburbs in search of cleaner air and a greener environment, beyond the smoke and grime of the city.

Steam-hauled passenger trains were running by September 1879 between Victoria and Bolton Street, the 1914 timetable showing that 60 trains ran daily between the two places. Initially four-wheel coaches were used on the services and within six years or so they had been displaced by six wheel stock. Shortly before the decision to electrify the route, bogie coaches began to appear, the six-coach trains worked now by Aspinall 2-4-2 tanks. Despite the comprehensive service and the construction of convenient intermediate stations, the public deserted the railway in preference to the electric trams which could convey passengers more cheaply, door to door, albeit more slowly than trains. In Manchester's case, a radial tram network had developed by 1910, the so-called 'electric star', starting at the city centre and radiating out in all directions. Whitefield, six miles out of the city centre could be reached by electric tram in about forty minutes by 1905. The cost of the same journey in 1915 by tram was 1 penny per 3 miles. The electrification of trams generated an expansion of urban mobility: in 1881, 18 journeys had been made by tram per capita; this had risen to 38 journeys by 1891, 56 journeys in 1901 (the year of electrification) and 157 journeys by 1911.

It was against this background and the consequent fall in rail receipts between 1900 and 1903 that the LYR was stimulated into considering electric traction on its Bury to Holcombe Brook line and later on the Manchester to Bury service.

The LYR decided to proceed with the Manchester to Bury scheme in December 1913, proposing a frequent service over a third-rail system working at 1,200 volts dc. The estimated cost was set at £220,000, a

Four five-car units stabled at Buckley Wells between duties in early LMS days. This is the high-tension end of the units i.e. the only end to be fitted with a destination blind. *Authors collection.*

An official photograph of Holcombe Brook stock, comprising motor coach No.3501 and trailer car No.3601, both in pristine condition at Tottington Junction. The former, with its sister 3500, was given Diagram 133 and fitted with twin pantographs to pick up current for its 250 h.p. motors. Trailers 3601 and 3600 (Diagram 134) could seat 85 passengers, 10 more than the motor units. After the conversion of the line to 1200v, these vehicles were given LMS numbers and modified so that the set of four became diesel powered. On the 25th July 1928 the set was put to work between Blackpool Central and Lytham. After April 1929 the four-some disappeared from railway service. *F.Collinge coll.*

large sum, but Aspinall convinced the LYR Board that the cost was well worth it in order to win back custom from the ever-increasing scope of electric trams. Once again, Aspinall was the leading figure in the proposed scheme, and again Dick, Kerr & Co.Ltd were appointed the electrical contractors with the LYR manufacturing its own rolling stock and bogies. Aspinall in 1915 was satisfied with the technical advances which had been made in electric-traction since the inauguration of the Liverpool to Southport line. The decision not to apply the overhead catenary system as used on the Holcombe Brook Branch was partly due to these technical advances in third-rail traction and to the lack of clearance for the catenary and pick-up apparatus under several bridges.

The decision to employ 1,200 volts sprang from a compromise between a desire to obtain the advantages of a high voltage (actually the highest permissible voltage in Britain using a third conductor rail) and yet be reasonably safe to track workers and other staff. To this end Aspinall designed a side contact shoe (patent No. 901 of 1914) which was pressed against the third rail by a 25lb spring, the top surface of which was protected from snow and dirt by a casing of fire-resistant Jarrah wood. The 60 feet sections of live rail were mounted outside the running rail on the same sleepers and alternated in their position relative to points and station platforms. The third rail was supplied by the Shelton Iron, Steel & Coal Co.Ltd of Stoke-on-Trent. The third-rail insulators were made of white vitrified and glazed porcelain, measuring 6$^{1}/_{8}$ inches in height, spaced 12 feet along the rail. The rails were bonded by two strips of flexible copper to afford good conductivity and where gaps occured at the ends of the live rail, the latter was ramped so

that the pick-up shoes were received smoothly. A fourth rail, acting as a negative return, was originally placed equidistant between the running lines, but this was eventually removed. A short section of fourth rail was reported in September 1960 to have survived on the spur between Radcliffe North Junction to Radcliffe West Junction.

Advances in electrical engineering in the early years of the 20th century were noteworthy. Power for the line was supplied by the LYR's own power station south of Clifton Junction and distributed from there to substations at Radcliffe and Manchester Victoria. The building alone cost in excess of £40,000 and was completed by the middle of 1915. Two generating sets were installed with room for a third if the envisaged electrification of the Oldham route had come about. Only one turbo-generator was required at any one time, any overload at rush-hours being handled by 1,200 volt batteries housed in the two substations. The location of the power station was some distance from the electrified line, but satisfied other criteria. The building stood on level ground at the foot of an embankment which carried the Clifton Jct to Bury line.

Coal was brought to Clifton Junction in specially built steel hopper wagons which were self discharging and were run over coal bunkers built above the power stations boilers. Some twenty two of these wagons were constructed for the service and were based on a design used already by the L&Y for its services to Formby power station. An electric locomotive was supplied (one of only two owned by the L&Y), being specially built for the Clifton Junction site and delivered from Horwich in July 1917. The small 36 h.p. locomotive (actually run off batteries) could haul three of the 20 ton coal wagons and replaced a

The 'rotary building' of Radcliffe sub-station in October 1972. This robust building originally housed three 1,000kw rotary convertors, other control gear, a workshop and a 10 tons hand travelling crane, in connection with the LYR's third rail system. The building measured 118 feet x 54 feet and stood adjacent to the Up line between the North and West Junctions of the West Fork and the Bolton - Bury canal. The lower part of the building, with a twin northlight roof, housed a bank of batteries used as an auxiliary power supply in case of emergency. This attached portion had been demolished long before the Second World War. In this view we are facing the eastern gable end with its wooden canopy over the main entrance. The section of track in the foreground is the former up line. All that remains today are the foundations, remnants of brickwork and two sets of standard gauge rails which entered the building at right-angles to the up line. *Tom Wray.*

number of electric capstans previously used.

Nearby was the Manchester, Bolton & Bury Canal which provided cooling water. Two main feeder lines conveyed the high-tension power from Clifton power station: the north line, 4 miles long, ran from the power station to Radcliffe substation; the south line, some half a mile longer, conveyed power to Manchester Victoria via Pendleton. Such technical abilities for 1916 were extolled in the January issue of *The Tramway and Tramway World* of 1916:

"Both feeds are of the same capacity, and consist of overhead conductors, of three cables in duplicate, and three-core cables, paper insulated, lead-covered and armoured with galvanised wires".

From the power station, power was transmitted along the track by cables strung on H-poles, with a standard span of 75 yards.

"The H-poles consist of two fir poles 10" diameter six feet from the butt. The cross-arms carrying the insulators are of channel iron 4" x 2" x ¹/₂" clipped on to the pole. The pole is braced with wooden straps and bolts, but no anchor stays are used except at points where the line makes an angle".

In congested area, such as stations, goods yards and turnouts, the H-poles were substituted by three-core cables carried on short stumps and brackets.

Electricity was fed to the track from both substations, this being done by using short-length feeders. There were no other supplementary feeders used between the substations. All this was state-of-the-art electrical engineering in 1916 and a great credit to Messrs Aspinall, Hughes (chief mechanical engineer) and Rattray (chief civil engineer).

The ten-mile Manchester to Bury line opened for traffic on 16th April 1916, Dick, Kerr, & Co.Ltd having relinquished their possession of the line and handing it back to the LYR. The first electric trains in public use began services the following day. This was a sound achievement

bearing in mind the problems of labour shortage and the delayed production of rolling stock, both due to the War. At first, steam trains ran the service in conjunction with electric trains, but the former were gradually phased out as the electric cars were delivered.

The journey time between Bury and Manchester was cut from 29 minutes (by steam) to 22 minutes (by electrics), a major favourable feature of the service, along with the high frequency of trains. Journey times (in minutes) between Bury and Manchester with intermediate station times was as follows:

From Bury to:	Stm	Elec	To Bury from:	Stm	Elec
Radcliffe	5	4	Victoria	32	24
Whitfield	10	7	Woodlands Rd	25	19
Prestwich	14	10	Crumpsall	22	17
Heaton Park	17	13	Heaton Park	18	14
Crumpsall	21	16	Prestwich	14	11
Woodlands Rd	24	18	Whitfield	10	8
Victoria	29	22	Radcliffe	6	4

After several months of smooth operation, the odd gremlin in the works had to occur. The *Radcliffe Guardian* of Saturday 16th September 1916 announced to all:

"On Monday morning, about 5.30, an empty electric train coming from a siding to the Bury station, fouled the points at Buckley Wells. One line was blocked until nine o'clock. The electric trains from Manchester turned back at Radcliffe, and the Bury passengers were conveyed in steam trains, two of which were sent round the loop through Knowsley Street station, and the others were worked on a single line".

The final fleet of electric cars consisted of 38 motor coaches and 28 trailers, all constructed at the LYR's Carriage and Wagon Works at Newton Heath, Manchester, except for the motor bogies which were

119

A specially posed photograph taken on the 22nd January 1917 showing the LYR conductor rail brush car which was employed to keep the third rail clear of ice and snow. A small oil-fired boiler provided steam which was blown through pipes on to the rail. Close scrutiny shows that there were two rotating brushes on each side of the vehicle. LYR 2-4-2T No.1044 is one of Aspinall's radial tanks, (short bunker type), introduced into traffic in July 1890, and withdrawn in June 1939. *NRM (Horwich F2199).*

manufactured at Horwich Works. The slab-fronted, flat-sided cars were, like the electrical engineering in general, of a sophisticated design as the following brief description shows.

The first complement of electric stock was completed in 1914, with later vehicles added to the fleet between 1917 and 1921. The February 1914 order was designed to cover all the needs of the Bury-Manchester services, three types of vehicle being designed: 20 third class motor cars; 9 third-class trailer cars, and the same number of first-class trailer cars. In 1917, more of the same vehicles were ordered with delivery of the last ones reaching into 1921.

The most revolutionary feature of all these vehicles was the all-metal construction, a body and chassis built as an integral unit which was quoted as "a weight-carrying structure as light as possible but very rigid and strong". The alloy steel framework was entirely rivetted and panelled on the exterior with sheets of aluminium. Each car was of the saloon type with a driving compartment at either end to minimise the need for turning or shunting. The floors were of galvanised sheet steel, covered with an insulated cement (Flexolith or Decolite composition) whilst most of the seats were reversible, first-class vehicles carpeted, heated and lit by electricity. The Horwich-built bogies were described as "wide bearing" to prevent rolling or swaying of the unit. Overall length: 63' 7"; overall width: 9' 4"; height from rail to roof top: 12' 4½". Weight of motor car: 54 tons; of trailer car 29 tons.

The usual formation was of a five car train (length overall 326' 3"; weight 220 tons) made up of the following units: Motor 3rd Class - Trailer 1st Class - Motor 3rd Class - Trailer 3rd Class - Motor 3rd Class, the latter being at the Manchester end of the train. Each five car set could carry a full load of 389 passengers, comprising 72 First-class and 317 Third class.

The LYR stock was life-expired by the late 1950s and gradually replaced by BR multiple unit stock built at Wolverton Works. Most of the LYR vehicles were returned to Horwich Works to be cut up, leaving only the aluminium salvaged for further use.

The fleet numbers of the various units was as follows:

LYR No.	Type	1st LMS No.	2nd LMS No.*
3502-3539	Driving Motor 3rd	14572-14609	28500-28537
500-513	Driving Trailer 1st	10933-10946	28700-28713
3602-3615	Driving Trailer 3rd	14669-14682	29200-29213

* BR added the letter 'M' as a prefix and suffix on each car.

The two-car BR sets were made up of a motor open brake (second-class) and a driving trailer composite coach. A full load of 178 could

A close-up of the current pick-up gear fitted to the original Manchester - Bury units. The side contact surfaces are plainly visible as is the wear on the contact shoe. Normally this gear was enclosed in a box formed from a piece of wood dropped into the slots visible on the protruding brackets.

theoretically consist of 16 first-class and 162 second-class passengers. There were 26 green multiple units plying between Manchester Victoria and Bury. Later liveries were blue and then tan and orange. At 63' 5" length, the vehicles were marginally shorter than those of the LYR, and instead of being slab-fronted, the BR stock had a driving cab whose upper portion sloped back to provide larger window space for the driver. The electrical pick-up shoe operated in the same way as Aspinall's design, this time fitted on each side of the motor-car's leading bogie and trailing bogies. The electrical equipment was supplied by English Electric Co. of Preston, the successor to Dick, Kerr & Co in the LYR period.

Aspects of operating the "Prestwich Line"

1. Regulations for working Electric Trains: Rule 141.

One feature of the BR electric stock was the telephone and bell communication between the guard and the motorman. The following code of bell signals was used:
Start train - *2 short rings*
Start train when propelling in accordance with inst.45 - *2-2 rings*
Set back train - *3 short rings*
Stop train - *1 long ring*
Shut off current when propelling - *1 short ring*
Notification to trip out the circuit breakers for setting back or that they have become tripped in running - *4 short rings*
Guard required by driver - *3-3 rings*
Guard leaving train to carry out Rule 55 - *5 rings*
(Rule 55, later K3) applied if a train had been stopped by a signal at danger. One of the crew, usually the guard, contacted the signal box within two minutes to remind the signalman of the situation.

2. Winter problems

The depot at Buckley Wells occupied the old ELR carriage works and was used to provide daily maintenance of the electric stock and general electrical equipment. In severe snow conditions, a 'ghost train' was kept running throughout the night, this being a five-car set which ran from one end of the line to the other in order to prevent an accumulation of snow about the rails. In 1947, a particularly bad winter for snow, the snow had built up very quickly into wind-blown drifts. The 'ghost train' ran into one of these drifts at Radcliffe Central station and was derailed. The normal round trip on this kind of work was about 35-40 minutes. The possibility of ice forming on the conductor rail was avoided due to the contact face being vertical.

3. The wooden cladding.

An important safety feature of Aspinall's third-rail design was the wooden cladding which protected not only the rail but also permanent way staff and train crews whose job might be to cross tracks or walk alongside them. John Scrace, writing in the LYR Society *Platform* No.28 illustrates the care which had to be taken even with the protection of the cladding.

"When the wooden cladding was damp, it would, however, give quite a shock even through the toe of the shoe if accidentally touched. My brother recalls a cat strolling too close for comfort to the live rail when its tail touched the wet cladding. It whipped round, looking out at what it thought was an assailant only for its paw to come into firm contact with the cladding..... which caused the cat to leap two feet into the air and then tear off down the embankment, no doubt never to venture on the line again!"

4. Control of Passengers

Such was the popularity of the new electric train service that in the first two years of operation, receipts increased by 80%, an increase prompted to some extent by the LYR's advertising campaign which described the northern side of Manchester as a pleasant and healthy upland country, yet convenient for the city. The control and guidance of passengers at its terminal and intermediate stations was paramount, and such guidance could be published on notice boards and in timetables.

"Passengers are requested to kindly observe the following which will add greatly to their comfort, and materially assist in maintaining the punctuality of the Service - *1*. To enter the cars at the rear end doors. *2*. To leave the cars at the front end doors. *3*. The First Class Car is always second from the Bury end of the train."

5. Electric train movements at Bolton Street station, 1959/60.

Bolton Street was, of course, the northern terminus of the Manchester - Bury line, and as well as handling steam hauled trains, it handled a constant movement of electric trains within the station confines. The following brief account was made by observers 'at the scene' in those changeover days when ex-LYR stock had yielded to BR two-car units.

"Bury Bolton Street station at which the electric services terminate has three platforms, two of them for the down direction and an up bay. In the off-peak period, the electric trains arrive at and depart from the down slow platform, but the other tracks are used during the rush hour. Electric trains booked into the down fast platform at these peak traffic periods have to proceed beyond the station to Bury North signal box where they are reversed on to the up main line to pick up Manchester passengers from the up platform. There are two stabling roads for four sets of electric stock just outside the station at Buckley Wells but the main depot and carriage shops are alongside the steam shed and are reached from Bury Loco Junction, the divergence of the spur to the Bolton - Rochdale line to the south of the station". *Trains Illustrated* September 1960.

The same observers, J.Hammond and B.Tinsley, regarded the Manchester - Bury line as the essence of unorthodoxy. The LYR five-car units were said to be the first of all-metal, no timber construction in the world, and they were the last pre-grouping electric stock in Britain to be replaced.

"An added unorthodoxy of the Manchester to Bury line is its obstinate refusal to be converted to 25 kv ac overhead electrification. The reason for this apparent anomaly, which will increasingly make it seem like an island of direct current in a sea of alternating, is that the necessity for expensive and laborious engineering work would have deferred for some years the already too-long delayed replacement of rolling stock".

When the Beeching axe fell on Bury, only the Manchester - Bury line survived intact, albeit with a reduced weekday frequency cut to 30 minutes, and a discontinuation of Sunday services. The last electric train to arrive at Bury left Manchester Victoria at 18.10, operated by electric multiple unit Class 504 No.M77165, on Friday 14th March 1980. The last service out of Bolton Street station departed at 18.30. Thereafter, all services terminated and started from Whitefield leaving the Bury end decommisioned whilst engineers connected the deviated line, using part of the Bury Loop, to the Bury Interchange. Buses were used to link Whitefield and Bury. The new Interchange station opened on Monday, 17th March 1980, the first early morning departure at 06.00 to Victoria operated by set No. M77173. The Bury - Rawtenstall line lingered on with much- reduced services. From 5th December

Bury Electric Carriage Sidings at Buckley Wells, 28th September 1958. End views of motor coach M28535M (LYR Car 3537) left, and First Class trailer M28708M (LYR Car 508). This is the non-high tension end of the sets.. With their life almost at an end, the vestibule connections had been allowed to deteriorate so that the vestibule doors seen here were kept firmly locked and out of use although as far back as the 1940s the use of corridor doors was discouraged. *F W.Shuttleworth, LYR Soc. coll.*

1966, the lines between Clifton Junction and Radcliffe, Stubbins to Accrington, and Rawtenstall to Bacup were closed. Lasting even longer, the east to west route through Bury struggled on until 5th October 1970, leaving only the singled line (April 1970) between Bury and Rawtenstall to provide a service of sorts despite a last-minute input of government cash amounting to £104,000. The slogan "No cogent evidence of social and economic need" accompanied the last passenger train from Rawtenstall to Bury, 3rd June 1972.

Bury Traction Maintenance Depot

BR built Manchester - Bury Electric Stock.7-day Exam Work Sequence
1. Check that the supply of blank defect forms are available in the cab of the motor car and hand any defect reports to the supervisor immediately. Record the milometer reading.
2. Check with supervisor for recorded faults. Special checks to be carried out and experiments to observe. Check the fuses on the control keys.
3. Check the passenger compartments, cab and interior fittings and trimmings, including the lighting fittings, for damage or defects. Check that emergency cupboard has not been opened, and that all other equipment is intact.
4. Examine the side and centre buffers and automatic couplers, including the springs and tail pins. Lubricate the impact surfaces of the automatic couplers, and central buffers. Check all brake blocks and change if below minimum size, recording those blocks which have been changed. Examine the slack adjuster linkage, brake rod levers and carriers, including the handbrake system, the side bearing springs, eyebolts, axleboxes, centre pivots and fixings for loose or damaged items, and check the security of all other slung mounted equipment. Examine the

wheels and tyres for damage and loose tyres, sounding each tyre with a hammer. Check that the white lines painted on the tyres and wheels coincide, and report immediately if movement has taken place.
5. Examine the shoe-beam and brackets, shoe-covers and catches, collector mechanism and shunts for signs of damage or loose or missing parts, and lubricate and remove and refit the boxes.
6. Test the operation of the E.P (Electro-pneumatic) automatic and emergency brakes from each cab. Check BC (Brake Chamber) pressures on each car with graduated and full E.P. brake applications and adjust the limited valves as necessary. Check the operation of the BC safety valves on each car on full emergency and replace if necessary. Check the brake-point reducing valve pressure in each cab. Check the operation of the D.S.D (Driver's Safety Device) from each cab in forward and reverse. Check the operation of the hand brake from each cab. Check the brake cylinder stroke and remaining slack adjuster travel, with full E.P. brake, and adjust the brake rigging if the threads are below the stipulated minimum. Check the creation of current air supplies, and check the air system for audible leaks.
7. Check the operation of the windscreen wipers on wet screens. Check the operation of the warning horns. Check the operation of communication bells and 'loudaphones' from each position.

LYR Instructions to Staff working on Manchester - Bury line.

1. Electric failure at power station or sub stations: In the case of complete or partial failure the Batteries will provide current enabling the trains already on the line to work forward to destination. (Inst 36).

2. Protection against fire: Sand buckets and extinguishers are provided on each motor car, and sand boxes are placed on the station platforms in addition to the ordinary fire appliances. (Instruction 44)

Interior of M28535M. The motorman's cab is to the left immediately in front of the vestibule door, the high-tension compartment on the right with access via the door with the metal push-handle. The seating at this end of the motor coach consisted of fixed and reversible transverse seats, those reversible in the foreground. *F.W.Shuttleworth, LYR Soc. coll.*

3. Snow and ice on the Rail: A conductor rail brush car is stationed at Bury Car Repair Shop for the purpose of clearing snow from the live Rail. The special train of electric cars or the conductor rail brush car must be signalled by the special bell signal 1-4-1. The brush car is fitted with sleet cutters similar to the collecting shoe of an electric motor car, and must not be run over lines where electric cars are prohibited. If the signalman receives an assurance from the man in charge of the brush car that the sleet cutters have been removed, he may then allow it to proceed on to a non-electrified line.

Every effort must be made to prevent the accumulation of snow where electric trains are stabled. Siding cut-out switches must be open before commencing to remove the snow.

4. Station staff and Equipment: Each station and signal box must have the following equipment:

1 hand hammer
1 cold chisel
1 pair rubber gloves
1 ¹/₂" spanner

1 ¹/₂" box spanner
1 wooden paddle
1 short-circuiting bar with red flag and lamp
1 section gap switch operating handle

5. Level Crossings: At level crossings the Live Rail guarding must terminate in the case of occupation or public level crossings at a distance of not less than 4 ft., and in the case of crossings for the Company's purpose at a distance of not less than 2 ft from the nearest side of the roadway or footpath.

6. The Live Rail: The live rail, its insulators, bands and cable connections must be kept clear of the ballast. Special care must be taken to keep the slot in which the collecting shoe travels free from ballast or other obstruction.

LANCASHIRE & YORKSHIRE RAILWAY.
CHARMING RESIDENTIAL DISTRICTS SERVED BY ELECTRIC TRAINS

Interior of M28708M. The first-class compartment can be seen to be less spartan than in M28535M. Once again there are reversible and fixed seats, the decor now enhanced with photographs or paintings of stately homes and coastal scenery. The motorman's cab is on the left at the front of the coach. *F.W.Shuttleworth.*

A standard set of five ex-LYR electric units leaves Bury Bolton Street station for Manchester Victoria, this is the 12 noon train on the 17th October 1959. The train has probably left platform 3 or 4 and has crossed the Down fast to take up its route on the Up line - first stop, Radcliffe Central. *A.J.Cocker.*

Another departure to Manchester in the summer of 1959. *R.J.Farrell.*

A brand-new BR Wolverton e.m.u. heads for Manchester Victoria on the Up fast line near Buckley Wells on 22nd June 1959 and is about to cross over the Rochdale to Bolton line. Worthy of mention is the style of the front end, complete with two windscreen wipers and distinctive head code box above the centre window. Note also the pick-up apparatus on the leading driving motor unit and the shirt-button BR emblem on the unit sides. The livery on introduction in 1959 was Brunswick green with cream lining and roof. These were the days before the use of yellow front ends, introduced as visibility aids to permanent way and other railway staff. *R.J.Farrell.*

The famous 'Monkey Bridge' spanning the Irwell south of Bury. British Rail Wolverton built electric multiple units glide across the bridge towards Bury on 28th March 1960. It is easy to see why the ELR bridge earned itself such a nickname and from the photograph it is not readily apparent that a pedestrian footbridge is carried between the narrow arches at either end across the river. *R.J Farrell.*

A Manchester-bound two-car e.m.u., fronted by driving trailer second, M77180, crosses 'Monkey Bridge' over the Irwell south of Bury, circa 1984. The central window is in use and a two digit headcode displayed, a feature which was to be seen less and less, the more recent use of the display area serving as a third window. *Bury Central Library.*

A Class 504 set in the livery of Greater Manchester PTE. This unit at Heaton Park on an afternoon service from Bury. *A.Swain.*

126

OBSERVED IN THE BURY AREA - items which were recorded as they happened.

October 1954. Jubilee No.45664 NELSON was seen on the 17th of the month hauling an Illuminations excursion between Sheffield and Blackpool on the line near Heap Bridge.

October 1954. During the month, the Royal Train left Euston in the evening of the 20th for the North West. After two overnight stays at Lowton, near Warrington, the Royal Train headed for Bolton, drawn by Jubilees Nos.45571 PRINCE RUPERT and 45584 JUTLAND, taking the electrified Bury Bolton Street line from Manchester to Radcliffe, and then travelled the Radcliffe Central to Bolton line from which regular passenger services had been withdrawn in September 1953.

January 1955. Bury steam motive power depot received BR standard 2-6-4Ts Nos.80086-90 and were put to use on the Manchester to Bacup service and also on banking turns at Heap Bridge.

May 1955. The evening of the 28th brought a series of excursions past Heap Bridge from Bury and Bolton towards the ex-LYR main line at Castleton. Pairs of double-headed trains were as follows: 2-6-0 No.42937 and B1 No.61123; 2-6-4T No.42654 and B1 No.61295; 2-6-4T No.42565 and B1 No.61377.

April 1956. New cheap single and return fares were offered between Bury and Bacup on the new diesel multiple units, said to have attracted three times the number of passengers in the first week of operation as carried by the steam push-pull trains - in 1955. To provide the new service, seven two-coach units were serviced at Bury. These are Metro-Cammel units powered by two 150 hp B.U.T. diesel engines. Each unit seated twelve first-class and 105 third-class passengers in what was described as a comfortable environment warmed by oil-burning heaters mounted under the unit.

March 1959. The Grand National excursion from Hull to Aintree on the 21st travelled through Bury Knowsley Street station hauled by B1 No.61305 piloted by 2-6-0 No.46418 having been put on at Rochdale.

July 1959. K3 2-6-0s were unusual engines to be seen in the Bury area but on the 2nd of July, No.61832 passed through Heywood in the direction of Bury with empty coaching stock, later to return light engine.

July 1960. Bury motive power depot borrowed Leicester based Jubilee No.45615 MALAY STATES for the week beginning the 3rd and made use of it for most of the time on excursion traffic to the Lancashire coast resorts.

July 1961. B1 No.61230 hauled the 11.35 a.m. Bacup to Blackpool excursion on the 25th. Earlier, the 11.8 a.m. special from Bacup to Southport on the same day was drawn by Class 5MT No.73061.

August 1962. Engineering work between Clifton Junction and Kearsley on the 26th delighted trainspotters as trains were diverted from their usual route by travelling via Heywood and Castleton. Authority was granted for Type 4 diesels to use the diversion provided they did not go through the Up platform road at Bury Knowsley Street station.

RAMSBOTTOM - Ramsbottom may not strike anybody interested in railways as once being a 'mecca' for train watching, but the following abridged account of steam locomotives actually recorded passing through the town for the period 24th July 1954 to 6th August 1962, may open a few eyes. The record is not a full-time, 24 hour day observation but purely a local enthusiasts record of what he saw. Remember also that the Bacup branch passenger service had been taken over by diesel multiple units in early 1956 and in March 1961 d.m.u.s had taken over those services on the Accrington route.

No less than 640 individual steam locomotives were recorded from thirty four classes, the class generating the largest number of different locomotives was the Stanier Class 5 4-6-0 (150), whilst the most prolific class, in terms of sightings, was as could be expected, the Stanier and Fairburn 2-6-4 tanks (127), one member of this group (42546 of Rose Grove) was seen on no less than 139 occassions up to March 1961 when its regular turns were taken over by d.m.u.s. Some 88 sepa-

rate WD's were observed and 72 'Crabs'. Ex-L&Y and LMS 0-6-0s tied at 29 each whilst 22 'Jubilee's and 5 'Patriot' 4-6-0s passed. Most of the other types appearing were in single figures with one-time appearances of some surprising engines, i.e. 'Britannia' 4-6-2; 'Clan' 4-6-2; 'Royal Scot' 4-6-0; LMS Compound 4-4-0; a York based LNER B1 4-6-0; and a J39 0-6-0. Other large engines include 11 Stanier 2-8-0s and two BR 9F 2-10-0s. Most of course will have probably worked through or to Bury and one can only speculate which types "got away" and were not recorded because they came during 'the wee small hours'. *From the diaries of Bernard Roberts, extracted from The Mancunian 1991, with thanks to the Manchester Locomotive Society.*

ALL CHANGE AT BURY - *November 1975.* Bury Shed was announced as being demolished in late November after being used as a storage place for surplus engines and electric coaches. The last occupants, prior to demolition, were moved out into the open: these consisted of redundant electric rolling stock, much of it painted green, intended for use on the Manchester-Bury service.

December 1976. On the 5th, the road bridge over the electric line south of Bolton Street station, carrying Tenterden Street, was dismantled. The bridge had carried the date AD 1847 and was replaced by a new inner relief road created by a concrete bridge.

July 1977. Work on the new bus/rail interchange station commenced during that month. British Rail stated that, on completion, the present station (Bolton Street) might be demolished. The freight-only line to Rawtenstall (East Fork) was to remain open for coal traffic.

November 1978. A new cutting, following the former Bury Loco Jct to Bury Loop Jct was completed, the old route being abandoned by a deviation northwards. The new line into Bury Interchange had to cross the Rochdale - Bolton line on the level through the centre of the erstwhile Knowsley St station. The new Hagside signalbox on the north west side of the level crossing had been completed but was not in use.

December 1978. Ballast trains had been working regularly for several months on Sundays in preparation for the new layout at Bury. In addition, spoil trains had also been in operation regularly on Sundays. During weekdays, occasional 'freight' trains, consisting of EMU cars were seen, the latter being hauled dead to Horwich for overhaul.

March 1980. The new signal box at Hagside opened on the 16/17th March whilst Bury South box, Buckley Wells box, and the old Hagside box were closed. The gates at Hagside were replaced with lifting barriers although on the 8th March, the barriers were not in use and the road was closed to traffic.

The last train into Bolton Street station was the 18.10 from Manchester Victoria and the last train out was the 18.30 from Bury to Victoria. During the changeover, a crane fell on the lines on the Saturday evening and was derailed for four hours, delaying the switching on. By 19.30 on Sunday 16th March, 25268 and a two car Bury unit left Hagside to enter the new station arriving about 19.45, the first electric train to travel into the Interchange. The service proper began at 06.00 on Monday 17th March and at 06.30 finishing touches were still being applied to the station during the first day of service. The Interchange boasted a loudspeaker system which was absent at Bolton Street, plus the ELR plaque from the latter station which adorned the entrance to the platforms.

ALL CHANGE ELSEWHERE - **Rawtenstall Coal Concentration Depot.** *"A huge coal depot which will handle about 80,000 tons of solid fuel a year is taking shape on a three-acre site at the goods sidings at Rawtenstall railway station. the depot will serve the Rossendale Valley and in addition to making an important contribution towards relieving road congestion, will take full advantage of the economy of operation gained from bulk transport and bulk handling at the distribution point. Hargreaves (West Riding) Ltd are responsible for the depot, which they are establishing with co-operation of British Railways. Rails and sleepers of the former sidings have been mostly taken up and new sidings will be provided. Coal will be off-loaded from high capac-*

ity rail wagons into bunkers and thence by conveyor belt to one of eight 25 ton capacity bagging hoppers. At the loading platform a sack-filling control will enable sacks to be filled at the rate of one cwt every five seconds and transferred directly to delivery lorries"
Rossendale Free Press 11th March 1966.

Diesel Train has Trials in Valley - *"A diesel train seen in Rossendale today may be a sign of travel facilities to come..... a light-weight diesel-operated train was taken to Rawtenstall station today when it made two test round-trip test runs between Bury and Bacup. There have been rumours in the Valley about the introduction of this sort of service for the district, but British Railways state that the trials have no connection with the introduction of such services. Those who saw the diesel train this morning were impressed by the accommodation. Excellent seating seemed to be allied to generous window space of an observation-car. quality Compartments giving head-on and rear views will probably have a special appeal for travellers. Also distinctive is the blaring hooter of the train. It is unlike anything heard from the steam locomotives."*
Rossendale Free Press 22nd November 1954.

Danger Through Silence? - *"The advent of the new diesel service on the Bacup-Bury line has since brought its problems. Rawtenstall Trades Council, for instance, at their annual meeting were concerned about the safety of pedestrians at level crossings. Their main concern was with such crossings as the ones at Langholme and Hareholme, which were unattended, and members thought that with the new service, the speedy acceleration and silent running of the diesels could increase the danger especially as there is to be a more frequent service."*
Rossendale Free Press 21st January 1956.

INCLEMENT WEATHER CONDITIONS - "Rossendale makes its own weather" may be an oversimplification but is nevertheless often borne out owing to the area's elevated topography which projects westwards from the Pennine Hills. Experience has shown that while it can be raining intermittently both south and north of Rossendale, the district itself has a very wet day, all day. In winter, Rossendale bears the brunt of winter snowfall the lying snow lasting longer, leaving the areas to the north and south comparatively snow-free. Low cloud often blankets the highest ground for days on end, whilst the valleys can fill up with dense fogs during the winter months.

Reference to past reports reveals that in winter (and in summer), Rossendale's weather can be freakish, seriously affecting communications, perhaps road suffering more so than railways, mainly due to heavy snowfalls. The winters of 1940, 1947 and 1963 are still recent enough to awaken memories of people who lived through them. The 1939/40 winter snowfall occurred between January 31st and February 2nd and was felt more acutely since conditions exacerbated the bleakness of war-time blackout and auterity all round. At the time it was compared with "the great blizzard of February 1933" which it overshadowed by its severity in terms of dislocation of traffic. It was also compared to the General Strike of 1926 which had also brought traffic to a standstill.

1939/40. The line between Stubbins Junction and Accrington was blocked by snow for a week, while the Bacup Branch was similarly blocked for four days. An observer watched part of the Branch being cleared of snow; "one drift was nearly 8 feet high". It was noted that LMS engine No.12981 ran tender first at the offending blockage, at full speed successfully avoiding derailment and forcing a way through. The section of line between Stubbins Junction and Accrington suffered even greater blockage. A Colne-Manchester train became snowed up at Stonefield, Haslingden. The same observer noted that double-headed engines Nos.65 and 2431 were trapped by a wall of snow 15 feet high. A down train from Manchester took six hours to reach a point 200

yards south of Haslingden station, where it became trapped in a snow drift. A relief train, sent from Accrington to convey the stranded passengers onward, itself became trapped at Baxenden, and to make matters even worse, two engines sent to pull out the stranded trains were themselves snowed up!

In a desperate effort to open the line, the LMS utilised the labour of 200 soldiers to clear the section from Stubbins to Accrington.

On the Bacup Branch. "It was Wednesday afternoon before railway services between Bacup, Waterfoot, Rawtenstall, Ramsbottom and Bury were restored to something approaching normal. On Tuesday, a light engine and a coach containing officials made an experimental run from Bacup but were unable to proceed beyond Townsend Fold." *Rossendale Free Press* 3rd February 1940.

As a news item, the 1940 winter snowfall was printed in the *Rossendale Free Press* on 10th February, having been subjected to censorship up to that time. On Saturday 10th February, a full-page feature announced that "These pictures will serve as mementos of Rossendale's greatest snowstorm for a generation." One of the half-dozen photographs showed Rawtenstall station with snow lying level with the platforms.

An observer recounted "a peculiar experience" on seeing semi-automatic signals (which had electric motors fixed to the foot of the signal post) continue to operate. "The drifts of snow had been blown so that the signal post was standing in a deep drift, the signal machine being covered by several feet of snow. It was very curious and interesting to see the wire from the signal machine to the signal arm working through the snow although the signal machine could not be seen." *The Great Snowstorm* Benjamin Elston.

In terms of duration, the 1947 winter, lasting through February and March, was even worse. The amount of snow was no more than in 1940, but the repeated waves of blizzards lasted for two months. As usual, conditions in Rossendale were bad enough to cause traffic problems. Roads, and consequently bus services most, probably because roads had to reach higher ground where they are exposed. The *Rossendale Free Press*, now free from censorship, printed the weather news as it came, went and returned. However, illustrations of the wintry weather are non-existent, leaving the local newspaper (the R.F.P) to sum up the situation on the 8th February: "Rail traffic in the Bacup-Manchester length was delayed up to 3 hours at the beginning of the week and workmen were engaged in keeping the lines clear. The electric trains between Bury and Manchester were kept running throughout Monday night in order to avoid the line becoming blocked."

Back in 1940, it had been found practicable to maintain the Manchester-Bury services with steam-hauled trains in place of electric trains. The R.F.P. on Saturday, 1st March 1947, wearily reported that, "After 4 weeks of snow and ice, Rossendalians awoke on Wednesday morning to find the district in the grip of yet another blizzard which had been blowing throughout the night..... Train services were not delayed unduly on Wednesday for only the 11.35 am ex-Manchester, and the 10.45 am ex-Bacup were cancelled" The same issue of R.F.P. reported that the River Irwell had frozen at Foundry Vale, Waterfoot, and showed a picture, dated 8th February, to prove it.

The conclusion of this discourse on weather and its effect on railways concerns water, this time of unfrozen variety. In addition to the River Irwell, there are numerous lesser rivers and tributary streams which drain the area. Past reports describe bouts of short summer rain storms and of days of incessant rain which turn the streams and rivers into raging torrents. the resulting floods occurred in July 1881, November 1895, May 1911, December 1936, August 1950 and July 1964 (there have been others since), caused by the overflowing of Rossendale's rivers which are confined to deep cloughs and to channels in densely-packed settlements. the impact of these floods on houses, industry, roads and streets was well-documented and must surely have affected the railways. Unfortunately, no mention has been found relating to flooding and railways: the effects can only be imagined.